Two Teachers in t

This new co-publication from Routledge and MiddleWeb provides a wealth of practical strategies and tips to help K–12 educators co-teach more effectively. Author Elizabeth Stein presents examples of different co-teaching models and shows how to cultivate a dynamic co-teaching relationship to benefit all students. Whether you're a brand new co-teacher or are simply looking to improve the dynamics in your classroom, the research-based strategies, vignettes, and ready-to-use assessment rubrics in this book will help you create a positive learning culture that influences all learners, teachers and students alike. Topics include:

◆ Selecting and implementing the appropriate co-teaching model to optimize student learning;
◆ Developing an effective curriculum that plays to the strengths of both teachers;
◆ Creating a learning environment that promotes self-reflection and nurtures critical thinking;
◆ Accommodating all learners by embracing a multi-dimensional view of teacher knowledge; and
◆ Providing specific, attentive feedback to help students take charge of their learning.

The book also features book discussion questions for each chapter so you can work with colleagues during book studies and PLCs.

Elizabeth Stein is a teaching veteran with more than 25 years' experience, spanning grades K–12. She is currently a special education/UDL instructional coach and new-teacher mentor in Long Island New York's Smithtown Central School District and a CAST cadre member. Elizabeth also writes the popular "Two Teachers in the Room" column for MiddleWeb.

Also Available from Routledge Eye On Education and MiddleWeb

www.routledge.com/collections/11190

The Genius Hour Guidebook: Fostering Passion, Wonder, and
Inquiry in the Classroom
Denise Krebs and Gallit Zvi

STEM by Design: Strategies and Activities for Grades 4–8
Anne Jolly

The Flexible ELA Classroom: Practical Tools for Differentiated
Instruction in Grades 4–8
Amber Chandler

History Class Revisited: Tools and Projects to Engage
Middle School Students in Social Studies
Jody Passanisi

Close Reading the Media: Literacy Lessons and Activities for
Every Month of the School Year
Frank Baker

Write, Think, Learn: Tapping the Power of Daily Student
Writing Across the Content Areas
Mary K. Tedrow

Two Teachers in the Room

Strategies for Co-Teaching Success

Elizabeth Stein

 Routledge
Taylor & Francis Group

NEW YORK AND LONDON

All About the Middle Grades
 MiddleWeb

First published 2018
by Routledge
711 Third Avenue, New York, NY 10017

and by Routledge
2 Park Square, Milton Park, Abingdon, Oxon, OX14 4RN

Routledge is an imprint of the Taylor & Francis Group, an informa business

Library of Congress Cataloging-in-Publication Data
A catalog record for this book has been requested

ISBN: 978-1-138-68998-5 (hbk)
ISBN: 978-1-138-68999-2 (pbk)
ISBN: 978-1-315-53723-8 (ebk)

Typeset in Palatino
by Apex CoVantage, LLC

To all educators who want to be part of co-creating meaningful, equitable, and empowering learning experiences within inclusive settings.

Contents

Meet the Author

Elizabeth Stein's career spans early intervention, grades K–12, and undergraduate and graduate level courses. Elizabeth has been a special education teacher for more than 25 years and is currently a special education teacher and Universal Design for Learning Instructional Coach in Long Island's Smithtown Central School District. She is a CAST cadre member and a contributing writer to *Education Week* and other publications. She is the author of the books *Comprehension Lessons for RTI: Grades 3–5: Assessments, Intervention Lessons, and Management Tips to Help You Reach and Teach Tier 2 Students* (Scholastic, 2013) and *Elevating Co-Teaching Through UDL* (CAST Professional Publishing, 2016) as well as the popular blog *Two Teachers in the Room* (MiddleWeb, LLC). Elizabeth earned National Board Certification in Literacy and is a doctoral student at Molloy College's Educational Leadership for Diverse Learning Communities Program. Follow her on Twitter @ElizabethLStein.

Preface

What's Inside

Many books—OK, most books—on co-teaching provide a "how to" approach to making partnerships successful. This book provides the "why to" approach to making co-teaching successful—which, in my opinion, must be discussed with more consistency and dedication to really make co-teaching work. We must start with the WHY. Why is it important to educate students of all abilities in inclusive settings? Why must we make sure that both teachers are active parts of the instructional and learning process? We must move beyond the "how to" so we may experience the "Why we must!" and embrace co-teaching as a living, breathing process—not a step-by-step recipe that all too often results in frustration. This book is all about the why—and naturally embraces the steps for how to apply structures and strategies within the view of valuing the human side of each individual in the room so that each student—each teacher—may have the opportunity to achieve his or her personal best along a natural learning and teaching process.

The co-teaching models are a necessary starting point as co-teachers strive to create meaningful learning experiences. The models serve as a well-defined structure that can shape and organize any lesson. Yet, the structures alone are not enough. An additional human side to co-teaching must be part of the process for making co-teaching partnerships truly successful—no matter what! Any partnership can be successful when the intangible human qualities are present with an awareness and commitment to valuing the thinking and abilities of each learner—including the two teachers in the room!

I have been so inspired through all of my co-teaching experiences. Of course my experiences include a wide range of traditional success stories where my co-teacher and I shared a philosophy, valued one another's teaching styles, and worked with ease alongside students. Yet, my experiences with the untraditional success stories—those co-teachers who did not embrace inclusive practices, or commit to a co-teaching experience, helped me to find my voice, strengthen my tenacity, and motivated me to advocate for what meaningful inclusive education should be. I hope the contents of this book will be the start of guiding more co-teaching pairs to co-create a solid "Why" co-teaching is and "Why" co-teaching must serve to advocate for truly meaningful inclusive environments—where every learner is valued. And it begins with a commitment from the two teachers in the room!

All the best on your co-teaching journeys!

Elizabeth

Acknowledgments

Collaboration empowers change. Years ago I decided to transition from an elementary special education teaching position to a middle school special education position . . . and my blog, *Two Teachers in the Room* was born. I am thankful for John Norton and Susan Curtis for their ongoing collaboration, support, and digital space at MiddleWeb.com the place where my co-teaching voice has connected with other voices—to strengthen co-teaching experiences.

I am grateful to my Routledge editor, Lauren Davis, for her timely, relevant, and confirming feedback for structuring this book—I am still amazed at how seamlessly we combined our shared vision for creating it. Additional thanks to Dylan Ford, editorial assistant, Natalie Larkin, production editor, Emma Capel, cover designer, and Holly González Smithson, project manager, for their attention and care in the creation of this resource.

With boundless energy I am always aware and grateful for my family: my best friend, my husband; and my beautiful children, who are at the center of my all, who serve as the source of my ability to balance, to sustain, to dream, and to achieve.

I am thankful for the opportunity to write this book—as an additional way to keep collaborations going across communities—as we all strive to co-create accessible and meaningful learning environments within inclusive, co-taught settings. Collaboration empowers change. And I hope that this book contributes to each reader's mission to translate ideas into meaningful action steps—steps that serve as a ripple effect that keep the power of collaboration moving the vision—the vision of consistent, meaningful co-teaching practices in schools worldwide.

Introduction

Co-teaching is defined as "two or more professionals delivering substantive instruction to a diverse, or blended group of students in a single physical space" (Cook & Friend, 1995, p. 2). Friend and Cook (2007) expand the view to dig deeper into a co-teaching definition through a description of the following three basic characteristics.

Co-Teaching Is

1. Two qualified teachers (i.e., a general education teacher and a special education teacher).
2. Both teachers have an active role in the instructional learning process.
3. A heterogeneous group of students (i.e., both general education and students with special needs) participate in learning in a shared space (i.e., classroom).

Collaboration consists of either temporary (a few hours per day, per week, etc.) or permanent (full time, yearlong) co-teaching experiences (Friend & Cook, 2007). But let's step away from the linguistic view of co-teaching and jump right in to some authentic examples that will illustrate the human side of co-teaching. As the following real-life scenarios are explored, readers can allow for the emotional side of co-teaching to unfold—and to bring meaning to the language that merely describes co-teaching practice.

Our co-teaching journey begins by setting a shared vision for what co-teaching looks like. Let's begin by considering co-teaching from three perspectives. My hope is that as you read each scenario, you will experience an emotional response that may range from outrage to hope. I invite you to consider your personal core beliefs as you connect to each scenario. Hopefully, each scenario will deepen your response to the question: *What do I believe to be true about co-teaching?*

Scenario #1

Marie and Joshua are two veteran co-teachers who have been through many co-teaching trainings over the year and have a solid understanding of all co-teaching models. Although this is their first time teaching together, they have been paired with a variety of co-teachers over the years. They each feel a sense of familiarity for what it takes to effectively co-teach. Each teacher holds firmly to his or her teaching philosophy—they feel they must, since they are always paired with someone new. Both teachers are ready to embark on yet another year with another co-teacher.

Your thoughts: Could this be a successful co-teaching year? Why or why not?

_____

_____

Scenario #2

Eric is a veteran general education teacher and Lauren is a special education teacher who is new to co-teaching. They are set to attend a training to review the co-teaching models. They are in the first few weeks of the school year. So far, Lauren feels like a visitor in Eric's classroom. She works well with the students, but has not yet found a way to communicate her teaching ideas with Eric. Eric keeps to himself; he is not excited to go through another year of sharing his classroom.

Your thoughts: Could this be a successful co-teaching year? Why or why not?

_____

_____

Scenario #3

Rachel and Christine are both new to co-teaching. They are coming into the school year with all the excitement and anticipation of this new opportunity. Although each teacher is in her third year of teaching, this is the first co-teaching experience for each. They are eager to learn and apply new ways of teaching and learning together to guide student achievement.

Your thoughts: Could this be a successful co-teaching year? Why or why not?

_____

_____

Which co-teaching pair do you most connect with? Take a minute to think about your own co-teaching beliefs and/or personal experiences. In the space below, jot down your thoughts—perhaps even create a co-teaching scenario to describe you or other co-teachers you know.

_____

_____

Gately and Gately (2001) identify effective interpersonal skills—specifically verbal, nonverbal, and social skills—as an essential quality in the development of effective co-teaching relationships. While keeping interpersonal skills at the center of the relationship, co-teachers must embrace the co-teaching experience as a developmental process with three stages:

Beginning Stage: One or both co-teachers are guarded. Communication is at the surface level. An attempt to create a professional working relationship exists. However, one or both co-teachers hold back feelings in an effort to just get through the year. For example, a general education teacher may feel territorial and/or uncomfortable with sharing the teaching responsibilities. The special education teacher may feel detached and excluded (oh, the irony!). The "unwanted visitor" feeling may exacerbate this beginning stage of co-teaching.

Compromising Stage: Both teachers have elevated the level of their working relationship through more open, ongoing communications. The special education teacher is an active part of the planning, instructional, and assessment phase of the teaching and learning process. Trust is established at this stage as both teachers cooperate with the ultimate goal of collaborating—which is the third stage.

Collaborative Stage: Both teachers are open, honest, and are willing to support one another with a high comfort level. Students benefit most from this stage—everyone (even visitors!) feels the inclusive sense of acceptance—where the voices of both teachers and each student are valued.

The collaborative stage, of course, is the ultimate goal of co-teaching success. Yet, it is important to be mindful that every stage is valued as a personal part of unique co-teaching process. Each co-teaching assignment is a personal experience that should be embraced. The process cannot be forced; rather, it can be cultivated through ongoing, compassionate efforts to co-create effective communication patterns. The collaborative level provides the added benefit of students learning effective ways to listen, communicate, compromise, and problem solve as teachers model effective communication skills naturally within the context of meaningful learning experiences (Gately & Gately, 2001). Friend and Bursuck (2002) identify collaboration, the ability to work with others, as the key to successful inclusive practices. Educators must share the teaching responsibilities with both teachers working together for all students.

Let's return to the three co-teaching scenarios. Each co-teaching pair mentioned at the beginning of this chapter has what it takes to build and sustain effective co-teaching learning environments. However, each pair must approach the experience in different ways.

Marie and Joshua must be willing to open their minds. They must extend their solid co-teaching knowledge base to create a new and fresh experience through connecting as a unique co-teaching pairing. They must remember that not only do they have new students, but they must also think as a new team and bring a new dynamic to their co-teaching experience. It's not a matter of just knowing what the co-teaching models are—it's a matter of *how* this particular co-teaching pair will design instruction for this year's group of students.

At which co-teaching stage would you place Marie and Joshua? Why do you think so?

_____

_____

Eric and Lauren must be prepared to connect on a variety of levels. Not only does Eric need to open up his mind to sharing his classroom, but he must also begin to relate to his new co-teaching partner in ways that guide him to see learning in new ways. Lauren must also be prepared to advocate for her role as a special education teacher. She must share her ideas for instructional strategies that could guide all learners in the room. She must not allow Eric's seemingly disinterested mindset to interfere with her knowledge of students as well as her knowledge of strategies that could guide all learners to connect with the content.

At which co-teaching stage would you place Eric and Lauren? Why do you think so?

_____

_____

Rachel and Christine seem like a perfect scenario—both teachers are over-the-top excited to not only work together, but to also work with the students. These two teachers must be careful to harness this excitement in ways that keep them focused and effective. They will need to learn the ins and outs of co-teaching as a team, while attending to their own personal teaching styles. The most effective co-teaching teams have two teachers who own a strong sense of themselves as learners and teachers. It is then that they may share, embrace, and extend the learning for everyone in the room—including the teachers!

At which co-teaching stage would you place Rachel and Christine? Why do you think so?

_____

_____

Let us return now to my hope. My hope was to elicit some emotional response from you. Perhaps you read with outrage and hope as a new or pre-service teacher. Perhaps you connected with some personal experiences as a seasoned veteran. Here's the place where you just embrace where you are at—identify with your personal connections—whatever they are. Before you read any further, I invite you to consider your personal core beliefs as you connect with each scenario. Hopefully, each scenario deepened your response to the question: *What do I believe to be true about co-teaching?* Jot the essence of your beliefs here and return to this after you read the book—it will be fun to see how your thinking and views on co-teaching have strengthened and evolved. This statement—right now—in the moment—will serve as a baseline as we commit to strengthening co-teaching practices and evolve as educators.

What do I believe to be true about co-teaching? Today's date_____

_____

_____

_____

_____

_____

You are now ready to dive into the book! I hope you connect with, challenge, and embrace how the contents of the pages of this book may guide your co-teaching evolution. . . .

References

Cook, L., & Friend, M. (1995). Co-teaching: Guidelines for creating effective practices. *Focus on Exceptional Children, 28*(3), 1–16.

Friend, M., & Bursuck, W. D. (2002). *Including students with special needs: A practical guide for classroom teachers.* 75 Arlington Street, Boston, MA 02116: Allyn & Bacon, A Pearson Education Company.

Friend, M., & Cook, L. (2007). *Interactions: Collaboration skills for school professionals.* (5th ed.). Boston, MA: Allyn and Bacon.

Gately, S. E., & Gately, F. J., Jr. (2001). Understanding co-teaching components. *Teaching Exceptional Children, 33*(4), 40–47.

1

Creating Possibilities: Going Beyond the Co-Teaching Models

Essential Questions

1. What are the co-teaching models—and how can they be applied to optimize learning?
2. How can Universal Design for Learning (UDL) support a successful co-teaching mindset?
3. Why must specially designed instruction be present in any inclusive classroom?
4. How can co-teachers take the models to the next level?
5. How might the planning pyramid be an effective tool for proactively designing instruction?

Co-teaching is becoming an increasingly popular service delivery model in inclusive schools (Murawski & Dieker, 2004). Learners within any inclusive setting comprise a diverse gathering of individuals who are placed within one class to learn the grade level content—together. Combining the strengths of the general education teacher and a special education teacher can serve to empower all learners in the room as they co-create options to make the content accessible and meaningful for each learner in the room (Friend & Cook, 2007). As part of a strong co-teaching relationship, various co-teaching models must be considered and applied with purpose and intention. Cook and Friend (1995) identified six models of co-teaching that describe the arrangement of teachers and students in this shared classroom. The models include:

1. Team Teaching
2. One Teach, One Observe
3. One Teach, One Circulate
4. Station Teaching
5. Alternative Teaching
6. Parallel Teaching

The first three models describe whole class instruction that is provided to all students. The latter three describe instruction that is provided within small, flexible groupings with each teacher facilitating learning in one of the groups (O'Connor, 2009). Let's take a closer look at the types of co-teaching models.

Whole class lessons (Figure 1.1) can provide a strong learning community of learners if the lessons are planned and implemented with care. The two teachers in the room must model a compassionate understanding as well as hold a solid view of their own thinking. They must guide the students in the room to also gain a strong sense of one's own thinking as they gain the perspective of others. Tables 1.1 and 1.2 share a deeper look into considerations co-teachers may discuss as they plan for whole class and small group lessons.

Figure 1.1 Co-Teaching Models for Whole Class

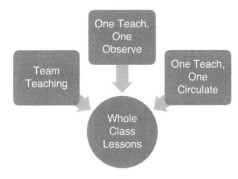

Figure 1.2 Co-Teaching Models for Small Group Instruction

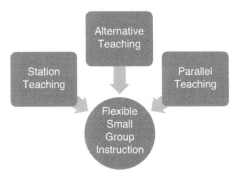

TABLE 1.1 Co-Teaching Models for Whole Class Instruction

Co-Teaching Model	When to Use	Examples of Instructional Strategies	Pros and Cons	Planning time needed
Team Teaching *Both teachers are delivering the same lesson at the same time. Each teacher speaks freely and instruction becomes conversational.*	Both teachers know the content well enough to each have a part in the instructional process. Both teachers have a high degree of comfort and are compatible with one another. When the teachers would like to model specific strategies and social interactions to demonstrate a successful learning process. Teachers then gradually release the responsibility for students to apply on their own.	Think Alouds (page 114). Teacher Modeling (pages 114–6). Guided Note-Taking (page 114). Universal Design for Learning Principles to guide differentiated instruction (pages 15–6). Socratic Seminars (page 114). Accountable Talk (pages 114–5). Cooperative Learning Strategies (page 115).	Pros: Teacher modeling and explicit instruction may be empowered by the personalities and teaching styles of both teachers. Can be engaging and motivating for students when well planned and implemented. Cons: The most interpersonally complex teaching approach. May be confusing or distracting to students.	High Level of planning time needed for the most effective outcomes. Each teacher should have a clear sense of his or her role and responsibility. Each teacher must embrace the expertise that the other brings to the lesson. Each teacher must be flexible in the moment to allow for any "teachable moments" to unfold.
One Teach, One Observe *One teacher leads the class in learning while the other teacher quietly observes one or more students to monitor students' performance.*	When questions arise about student performance and progress. When data collection through anecdotal notes or student work samples need to be gathered.	UDL Strategies (pages 15–6). Cooperative Learning Strategies (page 115).	Pros: Keen observation skills of students' performance. For example, teachers can learn about students' ability to: —initiate conversations and learning in cooperative groups. —self-monitor learning pace. —use problem solving skills and strategies. Opportunity for the two teachers to engage in peer observation to strengthen teaching skills in meeting students' needs.	Low level of planning time needed. However, it is advised that the two teachers confer about how this whole class will run to proactively support all learners. The focus of the student observation should also be discussed between both co-teachers to make sure that both teachers are creating meaningful connections between content and learners.

Model	When to use	Related strategies	Pros and Cons	Planning time
			For example, teachers can learn about their use of questioning techniques (see pages 27–9) as well as ways he or she interacts and implements strategies with students. Cons: One teacher is primarily responsible for the lesson.	Low level of planning time needed. However, it is advised that the two teachers confer about how this whole class will run to proactively support all learners. The focus for attending to specific students should also be shared to ensure that both teachers are focused on what all students need.
One Teach, One Circulate *One teacher has the primary responsibility for teaching while the other teacher circulates the room to provide unobtrusive support to learners around the room.*	When teachers are new to co-teaching as a pair. When lesson lends to the delivery of one teacher. When one teacher has a particular area of expertise on the topic and/or strategy. When the lesson lends to the need to support the process of learning for specific students.	UDL Strategies (pages 15–6). Cooperative Learning Groups (page 115).	Pros: Teachers can take turns leading the whole class instruction. Teachers can learn instructional strategies from one another and extend one another's areas of expertise. Students receive individualized supports during the learning process. Cons: May distract some students. Not helpful if students' attention skills is a learning goal. One teacher should not be the one who always leads the class as the other always circulates—teachers must share the responsibility.	

TABLE 1.2 Co-Teaching Models for Small Group Instruction

Co-Teaching Model	When to Use	Examples of Instructional Strategies	Pros and Cons	Planning
Station Teaching *Teachers create at least three different instructional activities. Each teacher facilitates the learning in each group while one group is an independent student activity. The students rotate between the groups to complete all activities.*	When a topic may be comprised of several activities to develop students' content knowledge and/or strategy base. Activities are not hierarchical and may be completed independently of the other activities. When instruction is review or additional strategic practice is needed. When several topics and/or strategies comprise instruction.	Explicit instruction for teachers to model a specific strategy or to provide additional practice to learn content. Strategic reading and writing lessons. For example: Collaborative Strategic Reading (see page 116). Sheltered Instruction (page 116). Guided Note-taking (page 114). Strategic Instruction Model (SIM) (page 116).	Pros: Students are given opportunities to: —be actively engaged. —move around the room within timed working sessions. —retain the information due to more strategic and individualized instruction. —participate, connect, and take active roles in their learning. —close personal achievement gaps by gaining knowledge and strategies to extend their abilities. Cons: Students may not be ready to work independently (in which case, only two stations may be created).	A moderate degree of planning needed to create small groups along with the instructional planning. Each co-teacher must take charge of planning one of the stations—and each teacher must share the lesson to ensure a successful flow of the learning process. Time management must be aligned with each activity to allow for smooth process and completion Each co-teacher must check-in with the other to make sure that one station is not running behind—and if it is, teachers should be flexible to work it out in the moment.

	When to Use	Strategies	Pros/Cons	Planning
Alternative Teaching *One teacher leads the whole class while the other teacher leads a small group lesson.*	When students' abilities of the content and skills vary greatly. When there is a high level of support needed for some students. When some students are working on separate skills, goals, or levels as it relates to each student's IEP and grade level curriculum.	Whole class instructional strategies—UDL strategies, cooperative learning groups. Small group alternative strategies: —explicit instruction —front-end scaffolds and back-end scaffolds —learning supports for pre-view or review to explicitly work on IEP goals as needed.	Pros: Provides explicit instruction that guides individual learners to close personal achievement gaps. Whole class completes an assignment or checks homework accuracy while the small group receives additional support, practice, and explicit teaching.	High level of planning time needed. Whole-class lesson should be proactively planned to meet the needs of all variable learners. Small group must be planned to meet individualized needs as it connects to the general education curriculum and each student's IEP.
Parallel Teaching *Both teachers are teaching the same information—they divide the class into two groups and implement the lesson at the same time.*	When lower teacher-to-student ratio is beneficial.	Cooperative Learning Strategies (page 115). UDL Strategies (see pages 15–6).	Pros: Fosters student participation in class discussions and activities. Increases student participation while keeping to a whole-class learning community feel. Allows for same lesson to be implemented with varying instructional tools and strategies. Gives each teacher an active but unique role. Groups may be strategically formed. Cons: May be distracting for teachers or students—but this can be easily addressed by monitoring groups and organizing groups so they do not face each other.	Moderate level of planning needed. Both teachers must plan/discuss the whole lesson—then each teacher plans for the unique needs of the specific group. Both groups could be brought together at the end of the lesson to share learning experiences and review.

Small group instruction (Figure 1.2) with two teachers in the room provides an exceptional opportunity for intensive practice and specific feedback that all students need to become strategic, resourceful, and confident learners. With lower teacher-to-student ratio, each student has the opportunity to practice more deeply and frequently within the instructional moments.

Choose Your Co-Teaching Model Wisely

It is important to not only vary the co-teaching models—but to also apply each model as it connects best with the design of each lesson. Four intentional steps may be taken to guide the best co-teaching model for each specific lesson.

1. **Know your students and know your co-teacher.**
    Consider the strengths, needs, and interests of the students (see Student Profile Sheet and Co-Teacher Profile Sheet in Appendix 2).

    All effective lessons begin with knowing your students. What are their general learning strengths? Who in your room has a strong background knowledge base for the content you are about to teach? Who are the students with strong listening, speaking, and note-taking skills? At the same time, who are the students who need additional scaffolds (supports to create meaningful learning connections)?

2. **Consider the content and context of the lesson.**
    If your content is laced with facts and strategies that can be broken down into groups, select one of the models that highlight peer interactions and student inquiry. For example, a social studies lesson that highlights the causes of the American Revolution may be effective through a parallel teaching structure to better support the students who have difficulty with attention—as well as all learners who will engage in a more personal learning opportunity. Each co-teacher would teach the same lesson, same content; however, each teacher may plan for different tools and activities in the process. For example, one teacher may use the SmartBoard to highlight visuals, while the other co-teacher may use iPads to highlight the same visuals—but with more student engagement through personal iPads. Other lessons may be better taught in smaller, strategy-based groups. For example, perhaps you know that some students in your class need explicit support with note-taking skills. In that case, station teaching may work best because one station could be a teacher explicitly modeling note-taking in small groups. Small groups also work well when you have students who do not read on grade level. One group could be the use of comprehension strategies (such as collaborative strategic reading or reciprocal teaching; see Appendix 1) to support reading skills. Whole class

lessons should be considered when both teachers present the material in ways that guide students to apply known strategies. For example, if note-taking scaffolds (supports) are still needed, but students are at a point where they are beginning to apply on their own, then one teacher could be sharing the content while the other teacher is modeling note-taking for the whole class.

The possibilities are endless!

3. **Consider each teacher's strengths and areas of expertise.**
   Let's break through the mindset that the general education teacher is the content specialist and the special education teacher is the process specialist. Yes, it's true, but these days, all teachers must be content and process experts. Each teacher must be savvy with the *what* they are teaching, the *who* they are teaching, and *how* they will plan and implement effective instruction. Each teacher must embrace his or her areas of expertise and be willing to combine it with the expertise of his or her co-teacher—and let the amplified learning begin!

4. **Consider your lesson activities.**
   What is it that you must teach? What must the students know by the end of the lesson—and what will the students DO to demonstrate this knowledge? Once you can answer those questions, you will embed your lesson objectives and content with your knowledge of students' abilities. You will then blend in the expertise of the two teachers in the room and create some truly meaningful active learning time! Make sure your activities are differentiated and align with learning goals, lesson objectives, and standards.

Planning for Differentiated Instruction

All too often, teachers select a co-teaching model and then say, "Great! We are doing what we are supposed to be doing—we are providing a variety of small group and whole class instruction—we're differentiating!" This is just a sliver of truth. Yes, implementing a variety of co-teaching models supports a variety of opportunities for students to learn—but just implementing a variety of co-teaching models is not enough. The activities planned within the small groups and whole class lessons must be specifically linked to the strengths and needs of the individuals participating in the lesson. Let's consider James in this scenario:

James's teachers knew that he was one of the five students in the class who needed support with decoding and reading comprehension in this sixth grade classroom. The two teachers decided to plan for station teaching for a lesson on learning the use of hieroglyphs as a form of communication, record keeping, and as a means of preserving and passing down history. The first station required students to read a short passage to learn how hieroglyphs were used to record history and promote power for the pharaohs in Ancient Egypt. The second stations required students to make comparisons between modern day text messaging techniques and the use of hieroglyphs as a form of communication. After an engaging exploration of this comparison, students needed to write a brief summary of the similarities and differences between the two forms of communication. The third station was an independent station where students practiced using hieroglyphs to create their own messages. There were many tools to support this independent station—such as visual charts, iPads, and visual modeled example of messages.

Simply forming these small groups is not enough. Forming groups alone does not support the decoding and comprehension needs of James and the others. Yet, all too often, teachers do not further differentiate the activities within these small groups to allow for students like James to build his repertoire of strategies to read independently. For instance, some teachers at station one may choose to read the text to the group—but how does that support the goal of having the students reading and comprehending independently? Others may pair the students to read together—which is great—but still, how does this support closing James's personal gap for reading grade level texts? It doesn't. Further supports must be in place. For example, the teacher could incorporate a chunking technique that breaks the text into sections. As the students read each section, the group summarizes key points through discussion. Because each student would have his own copy, James could mark up the text to guide his decoding comprehension. He could circle challenging words, and he could jot down notes he gains by participating in the discussion. The teacher could also frontload the vocabulary (see Appendix 1 for specific strategies) as a preview to extend James's background and word knowledge. In addition, if the two teachers feel that more supports are needed, students could have the choice to independently read the text on an iPad, using text-to-speech as needed.

When planning for differentiation, teachers must be ever so careful to approach it from the right angle. If the focus is on "fixing the child"; for example, fixing James's decoding and comprehension deficits, then the lesson will not be truly accessible to him or to the class as a whole. It is when the two teachers focus on "fixing the curriculum" that all students in the room will have access to create meaningful connections between their abilities and the curriculum. When we plan for differentiation in a proactive manner—by eliminating barriers in the learning environment and curriculum—we are expanding a well-needed view of Universal Design for Learning (UDL).

Embracing a Universal Design for Learning Mindset

Research in neuroscience has shown that there is the "myth of the average learner." Dr. Todd Rose serves on the faculty at the Harvard Graduate School of Education. He teaches Educational Neuroscience, and he is the co-founder of Project Variability—an organization that supports research and advocacy for the emerging science of human individuality. Dr. Rose is also the author of *Square Peg: My Story and What It Means for Raising Visionaries, Innovators, and Out-of-the-Box Thinkers* (2013). Dr. Rose's work with Universal Design for Learning clearly demonstrates that the "normal" or "average" brain just doesn't exist. What does exist is learner variability: the fact that in any classroom—any grade—any subject—anywhere—there are learners with variable needs. That is, students with disabilities, English Language Learners, and gifted and talented students are a *part of* this already natural learner variability. So teachers should not be planning instruction as if they are a separate "type of learner"; rather, we should observe how these learners blend within the natural variability that occurs anywhere learners are present (and that's everywhere!).

Universal Design for learning is based on the findings in neuroscience that suggest three primary neural networks to guide our experiences (Rose & Meyer, 2002).

- Affective networks (the "why" of learning)
- Strategic networks (the "how" of learning)
- Recognition networks (the "what" of learning)

A Universal Design for Learning (UDL) minded educator integrates learning experiences that tap into these neural networks with an understanding that each learner's networking is unique with individual strengths. These educators weave in:

- Strategies for motivating learners' interests and activate intrinsic, self-regulating learning behaviors (affective network)
- Strategies that provide opportunities for students to express what they know in a variety of ways (strategic network)
- Strategies for presenting information and content in multiple ways (recognition network)

(CAST, 2011)

When teachers embrace that all learners vary in the way they engage with learning (affective networks), the way they perceive information (recognition networks), and the way they process and express their understanding of information (strategic networks), they will become proactive in the way they differentiate to meet the needs of all learners in the room—without unintentionally and adversely labeling students (Rose & Meyer, 2002). It is important to remember that UDL is not a special education initiative. It is effective practice for all learners as evidenced by neuroscience—and our knowledge of how all of our brains naturally learn in variable ways.

The UDL guidelines (Figure 1.3) provide a visual organizer for the strategies and scaffolds needed to embrace and reach the learning strengths and needs in any classroom. Strategies throughout this book demonstrate how naturally UDL may be considered and embedded in all co-taught lessons.

Figure 1.3 Universal Design for Learning Guidelines
CAST (2011) www.cast.org

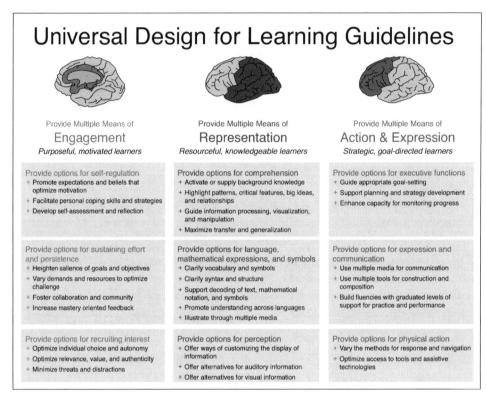

Taking our thinking a step further, we know there are students who need further scaffolds as stated on their Individualized Education Plan (IEP). These students are present in all co-taught classrooms. The scaffolds and promise of UDL are not enough. Enter specially designed instruction (SDI).

Never Forget About the SDI!

Specially designed instruction (SDI) must be present when students require more supports than the general universally designed and differentiated instructional scaffolds allow.

SDI is a mandate under the Individuals with Disabilities Education Act (IDEA), the federal law governing special education programs, and it refers to the instructional strategies and methodologies implemented by teachers to support students with specific learning disabilities and other types of learning differences.

It is often the case that the two types of instructional scaffolds overlap. For example, teaching modeling, previewing vocabulary, and chunking a longer reading passage may be a scaffold that the two teachers in the room feel is beneficial to all learners in the room. In this case, if it is offered as a choice strategy for everyone, it is considered universally designed. Remember UDL is not special education—it is effective practice for everyone. However, if the chunking strategy has been introduced and only a few students still need explicit teaching on how to apply the strategy, it becomes a specially designed strategy for these students. In other words, we cannot dismiss the fact that just because we taught a strategy to the whole class our job is done. There may still be students who require further practice and explicit instruction before transferring and applying the skill or strategy independently (Stein, 2016).

Another way that UDL and SDI are different is that UDL provides student choice. Scaffolds are offered as a choice for students to engage and apply. When students need extended supports through SDI, it must be blended into the natural learning process—not just offered as a choice. Consider this scenario:

> The two teachers in the room planned an exciting lesson on the water cycle. Students were engaged in learning the process through watching a video, reading a chart, and highlighting the various phases of the cycle with a different color, as well as singing a catchy tune to guide memorization. These strategies were implemented for the whole class within the structure of station teaching.

Great lesson, right? Yes, it's true, it was a great lesson—at least for the moments. All learners were engaged and all brain networks fully supported. But watch what happens when the end-of-class bell rings. There are still three to five students who have not retained the key points to the lesson. On this Monday, they leave class excited—and sure they will do well on Friday's quiz. In fact, they feel so confident, they don't bother to study. Why should they? They just experienced a wonderful lesson in the world of UDL. The next day in class, the students are swept away in another lesson—getting deeper into the content—with some (but not enough) reinforcement of the information from the previous lesson. This was a whole class, team teaching model. No one knows it yet, but these three students have already moved on from the previous lesson. Their working memory did not have enough support to guide the content to move to their long-term memories.

Guess what happens during Friday's quiz? You guessed it. Most of the class does well, two students earn a D, and one student fails. One of the two teachers says, "We did what we could—they just don't get it. And they didn't study enough." The other teacher knows that these three students needed more. More time. More strategies. More explicit instruction. And she knows just the strategy that would work to guide these learners to retain the information in meaningful ways. They need SDI. But she doesn't say anything to her co-teaching partner because she thinks there just wasn't time—or that her teaching partner wouldn't agree—or you fill in any reason here: _____. The point is . . . these two co-teachers did not communicate their thoughts with each other consistently or effectively. They were swept up in the swirl of the pacing of instruction and the content that needed to be shared. And, sadly, one of the teachers was caught in the "we did all we could" mindset. Even more devastating is that the other teacher remained quiet.

Co-teachers must focus on what they can do for students. At all times, consider what instructional decisions should be in place to support students with disabilities in inclusive settings. Co-teachers must communicate and advocate for these learners—always making time for SDI within the instructional moments.

What Does This Mean for Co-Teachers?

Simply putting two teachers (one general education and one special education teacher) in a room and telling them to work together does not accomplish the potentially powerful vision and mission of co-teaching. Knowledge of the various co-teaching models is not enough. Co-teachers need to embrace a deep commitment to a co-teaching relationship, so students with special needs are likely to make achievement gains alongside their peers within an inclusive general education setting (Kloo & Zigmond, 2008).

An awareness of the varied co-teaching models is important—with the understanding to be intentional when selecting the right model for a specific lesson. As co-teachers commit to ongoing collaborations, they will find a way to seamlessly plan, vary, and implement lessons that meet the needs of the diverse learners in their room with greater ease. Co-teachers must make the time to communicate their knowledge of students' strengths and needs along with sharing their own teaching styles and areas of expertise. Each teacher should be open to new ways of learning and teaching in order to make co-teaching a success in today's classrooms.

Taking the Co-Teaching Models to the Next Level

Vaughn, Schumm, and Arguelles (1997) suggested five alternative co-teaching models that extend beyond the basic awareness of the co-teaching structures. The following alternatives provide an opportunity for co-teachers to get creative, adding their personalities and their personal philosophy of teaching into the flow of a meaningful learning process. In addition, these alternatives can do wonders to ensuring that both teachers are actively involved in the instructional process each day. So open up your minds . . . and be ready to adapt, extend, and transform your thinking into action steps within your classrooms. The following alternative models are similar to the basic co-teaching models, yet add the mission to ensure that both teachers are intentionally and purposefully active.

> **Five Alternative Co-Teaching Models (adapted from Vaughn, Schumm, & Arguelles, 1997):**
>
> 1. **One Group—One Lead Teacher, One Teacher "Teaching on Purpose" (Similar to One Teach, One Circulate)**
>   Both teachers engage in active, meaningful roles. The two teachers use the planning pyramid (Schumm, Vaughn, & Leavell, 1994) (see Figure 1.4) to

proactively plan lesson objectives as they connect with the variable learners in their room. Over the course of the week's lessons, the general and special education teacher varies who will lead the lesson and focus on teaching the whole class, with a focus on what every student should know by the end of the lesson, while the other teacher serves in the role of teaching on purpose as he or she walks around the room to guide what some and most students will know. This teacher keeps a written log to keep track of students' performance during each lesson, with additional follow-up notes to inform future instructional decisions.

2. **Two Groups—Two Teachers Teach Same Content**
   The class forms two heterogeneous groups, and each teacher leads the instructional process for each group. This model is similar to parallel teaching where two smaller groups optimize student and teacher interactions with a heightened opportunity for the teacher to monitor students' learning. This model is a good model to apply following the whole group model of "One Lead, One Teach on Purpose." Following the two small group lessons, the whole class comes back together to sum up key points, so teachers may be sure that although their instructional processes may have been different, each group engaged in same content and same high expectations.

3. **Two Groups—One Teacher Re-Teaches, One Teacher Teaches Alternative Information (Similar to Alternative Teaching)**
   Students are assigned to one of two groups, based on their current levels of performance on a given skill or knowledge base for a specific topic. The groups should be formed based on skill level; be sure to incorporate flexible grouping (see "Flexible Grouping").

4. **Multiple Groups: Two Teachers Monitor/Teach; Content May Vary (Similar to Station Teaching)**
   Students may rotate among learning activities, or they may be assigned to one or more learning groups, depending on the lesson. Teachers have many options for their roles and responsibilities. Co-teachers need to:
   ◆ Monitor students' performance.
   ◆ Facilitate mini-lessons (10-minute direct instruction—teacher modeling) to individual students or small groups of students.
   ◆ Working with one group of students for the period, while the other teacher monitors the rest of the class.
   This group format allows for flexible, heterogeneous groups to flow within an inclusive, supportive environment—while ensuring that both teachers are intentionally and purposefully active.

5. **One Group: Two Teachers Teach Same Content (Similar to Team Teaching):**
   This model is perhaps the most challenging since it requires both teachers to be active participants within the content sharing and relationship process. It requires evidence that a high level, positive co-teaching relationship exists.

Each teacher builds upon the thinking of the other as they both share the content and are comfortable to be flexible, critical thinkers throughout an authentic learning process.

Schumm, Vaughn, and Leavell (1994) developed their planning pyramid as a guide for teachers to determine the importance of key ideas that every student must know by the conclusion of any given lesson. The planning pyramid's purpose is to design instruction that meets the needs of diverse learners, while maintaining high expectations and an inclusive mindset. Proactively planning instruction with the pyramid ensures students are not singled out, but rather experience a sense of community where each learner is valued for his or her abilities.

Figure 1.4 Planning Pyramid

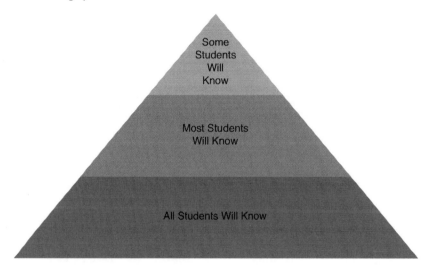

Some
Students
Will
Know

Most Students
Will Know

All Students Will Know

How the Planning Pyramid Works

Proactively planning with the pyramid framework in mind can take the philosophical stance "all children can learn" and translate this truth into manageable, authentic, actionable steps. According to Gould and Vaughn (2000), the planning pyramid has three degrees of learning (p. 365). Each layer in the pyramid represents a magnitude of learning. The base of the pyramid expresses what *all* students must learn and embodies the highest volume of the content learning. The middle layer shares what most students will learn, and the smallest layer will be what some students will learn. Planning with the layered pyramid creates the vision and sensitivity to design instruction with the knowledge that not all students are ready to learn all aspects of any given content area lesson. The key is in the planning. The perspective of each co-teacher could most certainly bring this framework to meaningful life—based on the specific students in their class.

Three Guiding Questions

Gould and Vaughn (2000) suggested three questions teachers should use to guide their intentional instructional planning (p. 365):

1. What aspects of this instructional lesson or unit do we want all students to learn?
2. What do we want most students to learn?
3. What information will a few or some students learn?

Additional question to ask yourself that could guide teacher planning: *What are the key concepts that all students must learn?* Co-teachers must analyze the lesson/unit and come up with the parts of the lesson that all students must know in order to maintain grade level expectations. Once the main concept(s) and/or vocabulary are identified, this is the learning outcome expected for those students who fall in the "some or few" layer of the pyramid. These concepts also show up in the middle and bottom layer as well, but the middle and bottom layer will have additional

Figure 1.5 Accessing Meaningful Learning

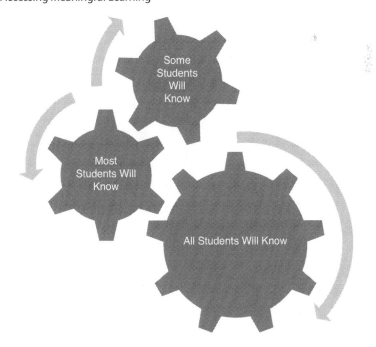

information to meet the growing need to enrich and extend students' thinking and learning as they are ready.

Do you notice the need for teachers to apply their own critical thinking skills during this important planning phase? Now consider that with two teachers in the room, co-teachers could most certainly power up the learning! As co-teachers use the planning pyramid tool to organize their instructional focus to meet the needs of diverse learners, they should also make sure to keep the standards and expectations high for all learners.

We will return to the planning period later in this book as we see how the co-teaching models and co-teaching expertise create the planning pyramid to flow naturally and inclusively to empower a community of learners within any co-taught classroom. As the planning pyramid is applied, co-teachers may easily find (in time) how the movement of the lesson—how each layer of the pyramid—flows naturally and productively to allow each learner in the room to access and connect with himself as a learner, with both teachers, with peers, and with the learning process itself. The planning pyramid may be the tool that sets the gears in motion for accessible and meaningful learning to unfold!

⊘ Co-Teaching Connections

Select three to five ideas from this chapter and share how you may connect each with your co-teaching experience. How does it connect with what you are already doing? How could you extend and apply in your classroom? What could it look like? What would the students be doing? Describe the role of you and your co-teacher. Share your ideas with your co-teacher—and listen to his or her ideas as well—and let the co-teaching connections begin!

_____

_____

_____

☼ Key Ideas

Broaden your teaching perspective. Consider the background and experience of your co-teacher in ways that complement your own experiences. This will set a firm foundation in any co-teaching relationship.

Choose co-teaching models intentionally and wisely. Consider the context of the lesson. What is it that you want students to learn? What will you have the students doing? What is the best way to structure the student's desks? Is this lesson best taught as a whole class, small group, or both? Team teaching; one teach, one circulate; one teach, one observe are the choices for whole class lessons. Station teaching, parallel teaching, alternative teaching are the models as you plan for small group instruction.

Co-teaching models may be blended together for any given lesson. You may decide to start out whole class using a team teaching approach and then move to a station teaching model to guide students to apply concepts just shared within the whole class lesson. Remember to design instruction in ways that provide opportunities for students to be active participants.

Differentiating instruction by considering the scaffolds and strategies as you design your lessons will meet the variable learners in your room. UDL provides the lens for fixing the curriculum through applying UDL principles and guidelines to scaffold learning for the variable learners in your room.

UDL is a proactive way to design instruction and remain flexible to meet the needs of each learner during any lesson. UDL serves to create access and meaningful connections to the learning goals for all students and often breaks down unintentional barriers that can amplify the learning process for learners. Remember that specially designed instruction must be applied to meet the additional needs of individuals according to his or her learning profile and IEP.

References

Anderson, L. W., Krathwohl, D. R., & Bloom, B. S. (2001). *A taxonomy for learning, teaching, and assessing: A revision of Bloom's taxonomy of educational objectives*. New York, NY: Longman.

CAST (2011). *UDL guidelines 2.0*. Wakefield, MA: Author.

Cook, L., & Friend, M. (1995). Co-teaching: Guidelines for creating effective practices. *Focus on Exceptional Children, 28*(3), 1–16.

Friend, M., & Cook, L. (2007). *Interactions: Collaboration skills for school professionals*. (5th ed.). Boston, MA: Allyn and Bacon.

Gould, A., & Vaughn, S. (2000). Planning for the inclusive classroom: Meeting the needs of diverse learners. *Journal of Catholic Education, 3*(3), 363–374.

Hattie, J. (2012). *Visible learning for teachers: Maximizing impact on learning*. New York, NY: Routledge.

Kloo, A., & Zigmond, N. (2008). Coteaching revisited: Redrawing the blueprint. *Preventing School Failure: Alternative Education for Children and Youth, 52*(2), 12–20.

MacDonald, E., & Shirley, D. (2009). *The mindful teacher*. New York, NY: Teachers College Press.

Marzano, R. J., Pickering, D. J., & Pollock, J. E. (2001). *Classroom instruction that works: Research-based strategies for increasing student achievement*. Alexandria, VA: Association for Supervision and Curriculum Development.

Murawski, W. W., & Dieker, L. A. (2004). Tips and strategies for co-teaching at the secondary level. *Teaching Exceptional Children, 36*(5), 52.

O'Connor, J. (2009). *Students with disabilities can meet accountability standards: A roadmap for school leaders*. New York, NY: R & L Education.

Piaget, J., & Inhelder, B. (1969). *The psychology of the child*. New York, NY: Basic Books.

Rose, D. H., & Meyer, A. (2002). *Teaching every student in the digital age: Universal design for learning*. Alexandria, VA: Association for.Supervision and Curriculum Development.

Rose, T. (2013). *Square peg: My story and what it means for raising innovators, visionaries, and out-of-the-box thinkers*. New York, NY: Hachette Books.

Schumm, J. S., Vaughn, S., & Harris, J. (1997). Pyramid power for collaborative planning. *Teaching Exceptional Children, 29*(6), 62.

Schumm, J. S., Vaughn, S., & Leavell, A. (1994). Planning pyramid: A framework for planning for diverse student needs during content area instruction. *The Reading Teacher, 47*, 608–615.

Stein, E. (2016). *Elevating co-teaching through UDL*. Wakefield, MA: Cast Professional Publishing.

Vaughn, S., Schumm, J. S., & Arguelles, M. E. (1997). The ABCDEs of co-teaching. *Teaching Exceptional Children, 30*(2), 4–10.

2

Essential Elements for Successful Co-Teaching: Theories, Tips, and Strategies

Essential Questions

1. Why is critical thinking a necessary element for teachers to embrace? How can co-teachers apply Bloom's Taxonomy to stimulate thinking for each learner in the room?
2. What does the Schema Theory tell us—and how may co-teachers apply to strengthen learning outcomes for students?
3. How can co-teachers apply the Depths of Knowledge model to any lesson?
4. How can the seven synergies of mindful teaching and co-teaching connect to sustaining successful co-teaching experiences?

Embracing Critical Thinking

Critical thinking is the level of thinking that takes any co-teaching pair from a "let's just do this and get through the year" mindset to a "Oh, the possibilities are endless for what we can do together!" action plan. Many layers of thought go into creating successful co-teaching relationships. If collaboration is the key to co-teaching success, then critical thinking could be the key to deepening the level of thinking and action steps for both teachers and certainly for students. Critical thinking has been a highly regarded, pervasive term within the educational field for over five decades. Despite its long-standing value, an attempt to shape a clear, consistent definition finds many disparate descriptions, each closely linked to the context of the sources that provide it.

To satisfy my own curiosity, I informally asked thirty colleagues for their definition of critical thinking skills. It is so interesting how easily their responses can be categorized by colleagues' backgrounds. For instance, math and science teachers claimed critical thinking skills were the ability to problem solve. English teachers emphasized the ability to think flexibly and synthesize information across texts. Social studies teachers believed students demonstrated evidence of critical thinking when they put newly learned facts within a context of historical events and then summarize key points in history and how they connect to specific themes. Art and music teachers supplied an enthusiastic dose of creativity to define critical thinking.

Definitions are often broadly expressed, resulting in a sense that critical thinking is an intangible entity of human thinking (Petress, 2004). There have been many definitions of critical thinking that express the extraordinary abilities in the potential of human thought processes. Norris (1985) ventured critical thinking to be the ability to think rationally in forming one's belief systems. Elder and Paul (1994) theorized that critical thinking was primarily metacognitive resulting in the ability of a person to take charge of their own thinking. Harris and Hodges (1995) posited critical thinking to be the skill of exercising judgment while reading, analyzing, evaluating a text.

Regardless of one's understanding and contextual applications of critical thinking skills, the focus to embrace the theory primarily began when Bloom et al. (1956) offered a hierarchy of leveled thinking skills that moves from literal to more inferential thinking abilities. According to Bloom, the human mind has the ability to remember facts, comprehend meaning, apply knowledge, make judgments by evaluating information, and combine facts by synthesizing and creating new understandings (Duron, Limbach, & Waugh, 2006). Bloom's Taxonomy continues to permeate instructional planning and strategic implementations within the teaching profession.

Anderson, Krathwohl, and Bloom (2001) have revised the cognitive levels to reflect the evolution of preparing our students for a future in the 21st century. The revisions in Bloom's taxonomy included first embracing the cognitive levels identified by Bloom et al. (1956): knowledge, comprehension, application, analysis, synthesis, and evaluation—and changing the nouns into verbs to more strongly express that thinking involves action. The revised cognitive levels embrace Bloom's original vision, yet provide the evolving mindset that educators need to fully embrace learning as an active process as students are guided to be independent, deep thinkers. The revised levels are as follows: comprehend, understand, apply, analyze, evaluate, and create. In addition, Anderson, Krathwohl, and Bloom (2001) inverted the last two levels of thinking to indicate that one's ability to create is the highest level of thinking, which incorporates all previous and valued levels of thinking.

Webb (2002) also embraced the original Bloom's Taxonomy to create a systematic four-level plan of executing critical thinking skills through his Depths of Knowledge (DOK) model. The four Depths of Knowledge include: recall and reproduction, skills and concepts, strategic thinking, and extended thinking. The Depths of Knowledge model was created as a tool for aligning the cognitive demands of instructional goals, curricula, and assessments.

TABLE 2.1 Tips for Classroom Applications

Strategy	Teaching Tip
Explicit Instruction	• One or both teachers model a specific strategy or simply share their thinking about a new concept. • Incorporate plenty of time for students to turn and talk to a peer to guide a deeper processing of ideas. • Peer modeling serves as a powerful way to engage students in a chance to participate in learning as students take charge of their own learning. • Peer modeling gives students a chance to engage in risk-free learning by applying a newly learned strategy or to share their thinking around a newly learned concept.
Make Learning Visible	• Making learning visible offers options for students to become aware of their own thinking skills. • Hattie (2012) explains that masterful teachers are not driven by the content or teaching a specific strategy, but rather they are immersed with a focus on evaluating the effects their instructional decisions have on their students.

The development and applications of critical thinking skills are acknowledged as primary goals in education; however, the evidence on how best to teach critical thinking skills remains undecided (Marin & Halpern, 2011). In one study, Marin and Halpern (2011) compared explicit instruction with implicit methodologies for teaching critical thinking skills. Students were assessed using the Halpern Critical Thinking Assessment, which comprised multiple choice and constructed responses to assess the critical thinking skills of high school students in low performing high schools in the United States. The results supported the benefits of explicit instruction as opposed to implicitly teaching critical thinking skills. The results show significant gains in students' abilities to apply critical thinking skills following explicit instruction experiences (Marin & Halpern, 2011). Making thinking visible is an integral part of the process when explicitly teaching critical thinking skills. Rosen and Tager (2014) found a significant increase in middle school students' critical thinking abilities when they were explicitly taught to develop Evidence-Centered Concept Maps (ECCM) as compared to students who were taught to organize their thinking with a basic notepad writing method. Dwyer, Hogan, and Stewart (2012) found increased student achievement when creating concept maps as they received explicit instruction in cognitive skills.

The research supports powerful implications for teachers as they consider the specific strategies that may be applied to create opportunities for students to think on a variety of levels.

Critical Thinking and Students

Theories and Practices

I. Theory: Bloom's Taxonomy

Designing instruction that fosters critical thinking skills is a necessary part of any instructional process. Benjamin Bloom et al. (1956) stated a fundamental difference between the knowledge level of understanding and the other categories of his hierarchy. Bloom was aware that the other levels—specifically, comprehension, analysis, application, synthesis, and evaluation—involved the cognitive capacity to manipulate the information learned at the knowledge level (Anderson, Krathwohl, & Bloom, 2001). Bloom's Taxonomy has stood the test of time to empower our own thinking and reflective practices well into the 21st century. Specifically, the revised taxonomy and questioning techniques continue to guide teachers to evolve with the times to support learning through carefully designed and meaningful active learning for everyone.

> **Levels of Knowledge**—The original Bloom et al.'s Taxonomy (1956) identified three levels of knowledge that served to guide educators to organize their own thinking through planning instruction. Metacognition was added in the revised version.
>
> (Anderson, Krathwohl, & Bloom, 2001)

◆ **Factual Knowledge**—The basic information learners must know to be familiar with a subject.
◆ **Conceptual Knowledge**—The ability to see relationships among basic information and the connections with a larger arrangement of ideas that enable them to function together.
◆ **Procedural Knowledge**—Following sequential steps, rules, strategies. The ability to know how to do something and to participate in methods of inquiry.
◆ **Metacognitive Knowledge**—The understanding of the levels of thinking and one's ability to think about one's own thinking.

Co-teachers may maintain the flow of learning with any lesson by mindfully incorporating leveled questions in a way that co-creates a risk-free, deep-thinking learning experience.

Tips and Strategies for Purposeful Learning Through Bloom's Leveled Questioning

◆ **Engagement**: Students will be engaged by listening, speaking, and/or writing to gain a solid understanding of the content, their personal views, and the views of peers and teachers.
◆ **Dialogic Moves**: Leveled questioning not only creates rich dialogue, but it is also a powerful source of formative assessment.
◆ **Response Focus**: Co-teachers may easily get a sense of what students have learned, understood, and applied through the weight of their engagement and responses.
◆ **Memory Boost**: Rich classroom dialogue taps into strengthening students' memory and comprehension as they become active participants in the process.

TABLE 2.2 Bloom's Taxonomy Application

Level of Thinking	Question Types to Spark, Support, and Extend Thinking
Remembering Supports literal level of comprehension through ability to list, describe, define, match, recite, and reproduce.	What happened after . . . ? How many . . . ? Who was it that . . . ? Can you name the . . . ? Describe what happened at. . . . Who spoke to . . . ? Can you tell why . . . ? Find the meaning of . . . What is . . . ? Which is true or false . . . ?
Understanding Supports comprehension and ability to summarize, paraphrase, describe, relate, and explain.	Can you write in your own words . . . ? Can you write a brief outline . . . ? What do you think could have happened next . . . ? Who do you think . . . ? What was the main idea . . . ? Can you distinguish between . . . ? What differences exist between . . . ? Can you provide an example of what you mean . . . ? Can you provide a definition for . . . ?
Applying Supports ability to solve, translate, produce, modify, construct, and examine.	Do you know another instance where . . . ? Could this have happened in . . . ? Can you group by characteristics such as . . . ? What factors would you change if . . . ? Can you apply the method used to some experience of your own . . . ? What questions would you ask of . . . ? From the information given, can you develop a set of instructions about . . . ? Would this information be useful if you had . . . ?
Analyzing Supports ability to examine, compare, investigate, take apart, categorize, differentiate, distinguish.	If . . . happened, what might the ending have been? How was this similar to . . . ? What was the underlying theme of . . . ? What do you see as other possible outcomes? Why did . . . changes occur? Can you compare your . . . with that presented in . . . ? Can you explain what must have happened when . . . ? What are some of the problems of . . . ? Can you distinguish between . . . ? What were some of the motives behind . . . ? What was the turning point in the game? What was the problem with . . . ?
Evaluating Supports the ability to critique, defend, justify, judge, decide, debate, and justify.	Is there a better solution to . . . ? Judge the value of . . . Can you defend your position about . . . ? Do you think . . . is a good or a bad thing? How would you have handled . . . ? What changes to . . . would you recommend? Do you believe . . . ? Are you a . . . person? How would you feel if . . . ? How effective are . . . ? What do you think about . . . ?
Creating Supports ability to invent, innovate, hypothesize, forecast, originate, add to, devise, construct, predict, design.	Can you design a . . . to . . . ? Why not compose a song about . . . ? Can you see a possible solution to . . . ? If you had access to all resources how would you deal with . . . ? Why don't you devise your own way to deal with . . . ? What would happen if . . . ? How many ways can you . . . ? Can you create new and unusual uses for . . . ?

◆ **Peer Talking Moves**: Incorporate peer collaboration through a turn and talk to a partner next to you. You may also create opportunities for students to initiate individual and collaborative thinking in response to new information by having students get up and walk around the room to connect with other peers outside their immediate proximity—supporting movement and building a whole class learning community.

◆ **Raising Each Voice**: Co-teachers seek the views and opinions of students to create the truth that every voice in the class matters.

◆ **Peer Perspectives**: Provide an opportunity for students to share their opinions and views as they seek responses from their peers.

◆ **Creativity Abound!**: Co-teachers can team up to encourage students to think creatively with time to tap into imaginative or innovative thinking.

◆ **Speculation**: Get students wondering, "What if . . . ?" Encourage students to gather the facts—and then consider those facts in ways that stretch their thinking to hypothesize and devise an idea and/or form an opinion that will be heard and valued.

◆ **Shared Learning**: Turn that "must do" lecture into a shared learning experience. Avoid the feel of a "sit and get it" (or "sit and zone out"!) experience. Make it interactive by incorporating time for students to process the material either individually or with a peer.

◆ **Track the Challenge!**: Challenge the level of thinking by noting on a tally sheet how often certain types of questions are raised and discussed. Celebrate all levels of thinking—with the goal to vary the levels to encourage deeper thinking through analyzing, applying, evaluating, and creating.

◆ **Co-Teaching Power!**: Make the most of the moments by modeling higher order thinking through your own dialogue with one another. Be sure to include examples and build upon the responses of students.

Speaking of co-teachers, let's turn to strategies specifically geared toward ramping up your relationship as teachers—with your students—and with the learning process itself.

Strategies for Co-Teachers

Critical Thinking and Co-Teachers

Have you noticed how many opportunities exist for co-teachers to develop their own critical thinking skills? There are many ongoing job-embedded experiences that promote our own professional growth.

1. **Reciprocal lesson planning reflections.** Seeing a lesson from two perspectives combines the expertise of two teachers who can empower the talents of one another through ongoing collaborations. Co-teachers can develop a deeper sense of self-confidence through peer feedback.

Through reciprocal, open-minded reflections, co-teachers can expand their understanding and applications of effective instructional strategies.

2. **Developing a mutual sense of presence.** Co-teachers can think critically about their instructional decisions and teaching moves within the actual moments of being with students. Each teacher can support the purposeful awareness and observations of students' behaviors. The process of instruction is a give-and-take between two co-teachers, which allows each teacher to become deeply aware of how students are responding and performing within the moments of instruction.

3. **Broadening one another's knowledge base**: Co-teachers have so much to learn from one another. Each teacher can support the learning process by expanding content knowledge and selecting strategic applications to invigorate the process of learning. Be open to learning and sharing—while modeling a true process of learning with your students.

4. **Resilient collaborations**: Co-teaching sets up the optimal experience to think critically about many aspects of teaching. When there are disagreements, resiliency paves the way, helping us keep an open mind about new ways of teaching a lesson, assessing student learning, and managing the class routines. The possibilities are completely endless—if we allow them to be!

As you and your co-teacher proactively plan for developing the critical thinking skills with your students, take a minute to notice how you can support critical thinking and deeper learning for one another as well.

Reflect

What is your experience so far? How do you develop your own critical thinking skills? How does this translate into your interactions and conversations with your peers and/or your students?

_____

_____

_____

_____

II. Theory: Schema

Embrace it! Activate it! Unleash students' full potential! In essence, schema theory is about the way knowledge is represented and structured in the mind. One's schema is built upon one's experiences, knowledge base, emotions, and individual level of understanding (Anderson & Pearson, 1984). Put this all together and we can understand each individual's ability and capacity for how he or she learns new facts and how he or she processes and makes use of the new information. Formative research includes Bartlett (1932), who explained that one's interpretation of the world occurs within an organized structure (schema) within the mind. A person's schemata is balanced between the external world and internal mental structures. Piaget and Inhelder (1969) claimed that the human mind is firmly based on cognitive structures that motivate and inspire one's intelligence. Moreover, these structures allow an individual to change and adapt to the environment in ways that permit them to integrate and accommodate their internal abilities with their external environment. Bruner (1979) posited that individuals construct new meaning and knowledge experientially—through authentic, relevant occurrences. Background knowledge is what forms the foundations and continues to shape one's schema. Background knowledge is a critical element in one's achievements. Marzano (2004) points out that much of what we learn depends on what we already know. Marzano identified two key factors that determine one's background knowledge. First, one's home and school life play a critical role in developing a strong background knowledge base. Marzano explained the importance for frequent rich academic experiences and the opportunity for an individual to process and store information learned through these authentic experiences. Educators have the important role of supporting students' experiences in building background knowledge. Schema is the key component of thinking in general. Background knowledge provides the foundation for future learning. The more we know, the more we are motivated and prepared to add to what we know.

Co-Teaching Tips and Strategies to Support Schema

◆ **3–2–1**: List three things you already know about a given topic, two things you'd like to know about or learn more about, and one question related to the key concepts.

◆ **Catch Sentence:** Give students the key word/concept that will be addressed in the lesson. Ask them to write a detail or descriptor with which they are already familiar that starts with each of the letters of the key word/concept.

◆ **Word Cloud:** Post five to ten academic vocabulary words that pertain to a given topic/concept. Ask students to turn and talk with one peer (or in small groups) to discuss how these words are related to a main idea or key points of a topic. You could also have students write a summary paragraph or sketch an image to depict the meaning and value of the words.

◆ **Carousel Brainstorming:** On chart paper around the room (or on paper that is passed around groups), ask small groups of students (three to four) to respond to a question or statement posed at the top of the paper. (These questions/statements should represent components of their upcoming learning.) After a short period of time, student groups move on to another piece of chart paper/topic, and read what has been written about that topic and add to or respond to it. Key reminder: Ahead of time, prepare the chart paper and the different topics, ensuring that you have enough "stations" so that every group is at one station during each rotation. These charts and responses can be used as the lesson activator, representing the prior knowledge and current understandings of the group.

◆ **Word Connections:** Students are given a grid of blanks (any number, depending on the age/level of the student and the level of complexity of the topic). Invite them to fill each blank with a word or phrase which they think of in relation to the lesson topic or lesson essential question. The words they record will capture the "gist" of their prior knowledge or preconceived thinking.

◆ **Dialogue Journals:** If students keep journals for the course, have the activating strategy be an entry in the journal in response to a prompt related to the focus of the lesson.

◆ **Word Splash:** Similar to Word Cloud, provide students with a list of five to ten key vocabulary words. (You could even have students co-create the list for an added challenge and motivator!) Students then create sentences to capture the essence of each word—completely relying on their background knowledge.

◆ **5–3–1:** Ideal for a think-pair-share or small group summarization strategy. Students summarize their thoughts around a given topic in five words, phrases, or sentences. Once all five are written down, they pick the three top key ideas. The group analyzes the three key ideas and narrows down the essence of those three ideas into one word, phrase, or sentence.

◆ **Remind:** A great strategy to use during class discussion, lecture, or reading/writing activities. Whether in writing or through oral expression, leave a word out (cloze procedure style). Pause to allow students to predict the word and fill in the blank. May be administered whole class or take a few minutes for students to pair-share or briefly discuss in small groups. Serves to activate and validate background knowledge.

◆ **Plus/Minus/Intriguing:** Provide factual and/or controversial statement(s) that are connected to the focus of the upcoming lesson. Have students identify the statements they agree with (+), the statements they disagree with or question (–), and the statements they find intriguing (I).

◆ **Reflect:**
1. What critical thinking skills do you notice naturally embedded in these strategies? Share one example—be specific.
2. Select one strategy to support the development of schema from the list above. How could you and your co-teacher share in the instructional delivery of implementing this strategy? What would the role for each of you be? Make sure you both play an active part!
3. How does this translate into your interactions and conversations with your peers and/or your students?

_____

_____

_____

_____

III. Theory: Depths of Knowledge

Webb (1997) developed the Depths of Knowledge (DOK) framework as a way of categorizing cognitive demands based on the levels of Bloom's taxonomy. The DOK framework illuminates the connections and level of reasoning needed to respond to an academic task or when responding to a test item during formal assessments. Webb's DOK levels may be viewed as an alternative taxonomy for describing the cognitive complexities required in an academic task (Wyse & Viger, 2011).

TABLE 2.3 DOK Levels and Activities

DOK Level	Activity Samples
Level One: Recall and Reproduction Locate, define, list, label, match, copy, state, tell. Involves recalling, recognizing, and reproducing information to work with facts. Simple procedures and remembering sequential steps and procedures are also a part of this level. A foundation of knowledge (and schema!) rests at this DOK level.	• Recall story elements: setting, characters, events, problem, solution. • Recall the elements of the periodic table. • Demonstrate how to simplify each fraction. • Describe the environmental features of an ancient civilization. • Locate places on a map. • Paraphrase the key points of a chapter.
Level Two: Skills and Concepts Infer, categorize, interpret, summarize, translate, predict. Think beyond recalling information and begin to synthesize, compare or contrast ideas, and think about causal relationships. This level moves a thinker from the "what" I am learning to "why" I need and want to learn about this topic.	• Explain the meaning of a concept. • Compare/contrast. • Create a solution for . . . • Construct a model or journal entry to demonstrate how something works. • Illustrate an image to show your understanding. • Write an explanation of this topic.
Level 3: Short-Term Strategic Thinking and Reasoning Critique, cite evidence, conclude, argue, hypothesize. Short-term memory and higher order thinking needed to analyze and evaluate information in order to solve real-world problems.	• Survey peers to find out what they think about a particular topic. • Create a flow chart to demonstrate critical phases. • Write a persuasive letter or speech. • Explain abstract terms and concepts. • Identify a hypothesis or research question and design an investigation or experiment. • Propose a solution for . . . • Make a prediction about. . .

DOK Level	Activity Samples
Level Four: Extended Strategic Thinking Initiate, design, synthesize, self-monitor, critique, conduct. Apply sustained strategic thinking over longer periods of time by synthesizing while reflecting and by conducting investigations to solve real-world problems. Thinking at this level is flexible to sustain inquiry-based learning and problem solving that often have unpredictable outcomes.	• Devise a new way to . . . • Create a story, song, or plan for . . . • Any task that requires a number of cognitive and physical skills to complete. • Considering the perspective of others through collaborative discussions and tasks. • Formulate a hypothesis and test out your theory over time.

Notice the levels and the verbs coincide with the original Bloom's Taxonomy; however, the DOK framework represents four different ways that students interact with content. It promotes a fluid process—where all four levels are important. The DOK framework is not a hierarchy that is scripted and celebrated as one moves higher along a thinking path. Rather, it is a process where each verb does not depict one level—it is the task that defines the rigor of the students' thinking. For example, the verb *describe* may be embraced at deeper levels of thinking—see Table 2.4.

TABLE 2.4 Same Verb in Different DOK Levels

DOK Verb: *Describe*
• DOK Level 1- *Describe* the different moon phases. (Requires basic recall.)
• DOK Level 2- *Describe* the difference between waning gibbous and waxing gibbous as seen in the northern hemisphere. (Requires cognitive processing to determine the differences in the two phases of the moon.)
• DOK Level 3- *Describe* the relationship between the positioning of the earth, moon, and sun during a full moon. (Requires deep understanding of the cause of the moon various phases.)

Co-Teaching Tips and Strategies to Support Depths of Knowledge Levels

◆ **Integrate project-based learning**: Provide weekly time for students to generate a question and create a plan to research solutions.

◆ **Embed habits of mind** (see Table 2.5, "Sixteen Habits of Mind") to provide students with the opportunity to embrace the disposition needed to approach learning opportunities with the tenacity and persistence to apply sustained extended thinking to solve problems and gain valuable insights.

◆ **Create a sound**: Engage students in a conversation about a given topic. Provide a variety of different instruments (triangle, shakers, bells, tambourine, blocks, chimes, cabasa, finger symbols, etc.). Have students create a sound with their instrument to depict their feelings before the discussion begins—or a sound to put the topic to music. Students could take turns listening to one another and join in an ensemble as the discussion flows.

◆ **Concept Maps:** Concept maps may be used over time to provide a way for students to gather and organize conceptual knowledge.

◆ **Read, Review, Create:** Share a short text, poem, or mathematical word problem or equation—ask students to create their own version as an additional example and to extend and generalize their understanding.

◆ **Reflect:**
1. Select one strategy or DOK level; how could you and your co-teacher share in the instructional delivery of implementing a variety of levels across a variety of lessons? What would the role for each of you be? Make sure you both play an active part!
2. How could you use the DOK levels to deepen your co-teaching conversations and your co-taught lessons?
3. How can you use the sixteen habits of mind (see Table 2.5) to strengthen your co-teaching relationship as well as your relationships with students and the learning process within your classroom?

_____

_____

_____

_____

IV. Practice: Sixteen Habits of Mind

Costa and Kallick (2000) identified sixteen "habits of mind" that provide an individual with skills to work through real-life situations. These skills equip a person to respond using a keen sense of awareness, along with intentional thoughts and action steps, to gain positive outcomes.

TABLE 2.5 Sixteen Habits of Mind

1. **Persisting:** Stay focused on task at hand. Follow through to completion—over time.
2. **Managing Impulsivity:** Think before speaking or acting; Embrace stress or challenges by remaining calm and thoughtful. Stay considerate of others.
3. **Listening with Understanding and Empathy:** Pay attention to another person's thoughts, feelings, and ideas. Put yourself in the other person's shoes. Tell others when you can relate to what they are expressing. Hold thoughts at a distance in order to respect another person's point of view and feelings.
4. **Thinking Flexibly:** Be able to consider the ideas of others and change your own perspective. Be able to think of options and make decisions based on considered opinion.

5. **Thinking About Thinking (Metacognition):** Be aware of your own thoughts, feelings, intentions, and actions. Know your words and actions affect others. Be willing to consider the impact of choices on yourself and others.
6. **Striving for Accuracy:** Self-regulate and check for errors. Think and act with integrity, fidelity, and craftsmanship.
7. **Questioning and Posing Problems:** Develop a questioning attitude. Consider what information is needed. Choose strategies to guide the process toward solutions. Consider the barriers needed to resolve problems.
8. **Applying Past Knowledge to New Situations:** Consider prior knowledge and experiences and connect with new learning. Apply knowledge beyond the current situation and moments in time.
9. **Thinking and Communicating with Clarity and Precision:** Strive to be clear and accurate when speaking and writing.
10. **Gathering Data Through All Senses:** Be mindful and present by noticing what you see. Listen to the sounds you hear. Take in the fragrance of what you smell. Notice the flavor of what you are eating. Notice the texture of what you are touching.
11. **Creating, Imagining, Innovating:** Think about how something might be done differently from the typical approach. Propose new ideas, seek originality, and consider novel ideas.
12. **Responding with Wonderment and Awe:** Be intrigued by the beauty in nature and all around you. Be open to the little and big surprises in life as you see others and yourself.
13. **Taking Responsible Risks:** Be willing to try something new and different. Embrace mistakes as a natural part of the learning process.
14. **Finding Humor:** Notice the whimsical, absurd, ironic, and unexpected in life—and find the humor. Be willing to laugh at yourself when applicable.
15. **Thinking Interdependently:** Respect the perspectives of others and work cooperatively. Be willing to learn from others.
16. **Remaining Open to Continuous Learning:** Be open to new experiences. Be humble and admit when you don't know. Welcome new ideas.

V. Practice: Co-Teaching With Maslow

Maslow (1943) created a hierarchy of needs that aimed to capture the complexity of human behavior and explain the reasons for any given behavior. Maslow's hierarchy, often depicted in a pyramid, has five levels. The first four levels are considered lower-level needs, while the top level is considered the highest level of growth and highlights more cognitive, intangible, and intellectual needs, which are considered the ultimate goal of achievement.

The levels are as follows (see pyramid in Figure 2.1):

◆ Self-actualization—includes morality, creativity, problem solving, etc.
◆ Esteem—includes confidence, self-esteem, achievement, respect, etc.
◆ Belongingness—includes love, friendship, intimacy, family, etc.
◆ Safety—includes security of environment, employment, resources, health.
◆ Physiological—includes air, food, water, physical activity, sleep, other factors towards homeostasis.

Now let's add a co-teaching spin to our knowledge of Maslow. Our environment, our desires, and our connections, and relationships with others control the first four levels of need. Our minds and our intellect control the satisfaction of the highest level, according to Maslow.

Figure 2.1 Maslow's Hierarchy of Needs

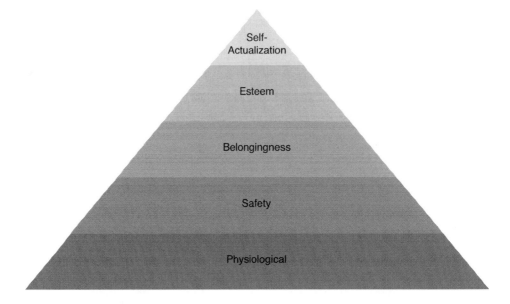

Reflect

1. Consider how you and your co-teacher align your instructional decisions with the needs of your students—how do they align with Maslow's levels of need?

_____

_____

_____

2. How can you and your co-teacher apply Maslow's hierarchy of needs to ensure a productive, collaborative co-teaching relationship? Be specific—what can you do tomorrow?

_____

_____

_____

3. Do you think you can apply Bloom's Taxonomy or Webb's Depths of Knowledge before considering Maslow's hierarchy? Discuss with your co-teacher and decide how this could positively impact your relationships with each other, with students, and with your ideas for your co-designed lessons.

_____

_____

_____

VI. Practice: Mindful Co-Teaching

Mindful teachers are educators who balance the emotional, intellectual, and professional side of learning within collaborative settings. They encourage collegial conversations where every voice is heard and valued. Mindful teachers speak honestly about needs, concerns, and celebrations in regards to themselves, their colleagues, and their students (MacDonald & Shirley, 2009). Mindful teachers become strong advocates for developing positive relationships through valuing the perspective of others. One's perspective firmly rests on an awareness to detach from a stronghold of one's perspective if the potential to become judgmental of others' perspective becomes a risk factor (Langer, 2014). As teachers develop a keen sense of focus and awareness for thoughts and actions, they position themselves to be leaders of change—where change is viewed as a positive cycle that connects the known to the new. For example, consider the following scenario where two co-teachers are discussing a lesson that has resulted in one co-teacher becoming upset at the other teacher:

Mr. B: I just needed to explain the powers of the three branches of government, so we would be set up for tomorrow's lesson.

Mrs. R: I completely understood that—I was just taking care of the students who needed more supports to understand what you were talking about—so I modeled outline note-taking to provide a visual of the important facts you were sharing.

Mr. B: I already had the PowerPoint slides as visuals—I have been teaching this lesson for years—and it always goes so well—I feel like you think my lessons aren't good enough.

Mrs. R. Quite the contrary! Your lesson—including your visuals—was amazing! It's just that this year, we have specific students who need alternatives to the oral and visual PowerPoint slides. They need direct instruction on how to take notes. As one of the co-teachers, I need to make sure that the students get what they need in the moments of instruction. I didn't think my quietly modeling note-taking on the side would interfere with you. Didn't you notice the active note-taking and listening that was going on in class?!

Mr. B: No! I noticed that the students were looking at you and not me—I noticed you stole my thunder!

So what is a co-teacher to do? Just stop modeling notes? This co-teaching pair is at the beginning stage of developing a co-teaching relationship (remember the stages from Chapter 1?). Mr. B. is clearly having a difficult time sharing the instructional space. Mrs. R. is understanding of that fact, yet she must advocate for her role as a special education teacher—and equal educator in this co-teaching experience. So what is a co-teacher to do? What would you do?

There certainly are no quick fixes to the scenario above. Sure, Mrs. R. could cause a scene and say, "Sorry, but I must do what I must do—like it or not!" But what good would that be for creating an effective co-teaching relationship for the rest of the year?

Enter a Mindful Teaching Approach

A mindful co-teacher values the perspective of his or her teaching partner. When conflicts arise, a mindful teacher meets the situation with acceptance and understanding— while gently inviting new ideas into the midst of conversations and action steps. New ideas are never forced; rather, they are gently, consistently, tenaciously entered into the scene. Ideally, if both co-teachers are mindful—life is grand! Everyone celebrates! All egos aside, so the learning pathway is clear! Yet, that is not the reality in all classrooms . . . so let's return to the question: *What's a co-teacher to do?*

For starters, a co-teacher must realize there is more to the situation then one's own perspective. Mrs. R. wants to support meaningful learning for all students. Mr. B also wants to support learning by making sure students get all the information they need. Their intentions are aligned. Yet, their ideas for how to get there are vastly different.

Here's how the rest of the story goes.

Mrs. R: My intention was to provide additional visual support—to guide effective note-taking for this lesson—but also, they're learning a structure for how to take notes for future lessons, so they will be independent note-takers in time. I never thought you would feel I was in your way. My focus was on giving the students what they need.

Mr. B: Well, it was in my way—I need kids to look at me when I'm talking—not you and your note-taking.

Mrs. R: OK, so what do you suggest we do?

Mr. B: The only thing I can think of is just give students a copy of the PowerPoint slides—so they will have the notes.

Mrs. R: I feel that would be enabling them—they need to know how to take notes—for this class and in general. How about you send me the lessons ahead of time—I could create a guided notes handout where I will intentionally leave out some key words. Students will have to fill in the blanks as they listen during the lesson?

Mr. B: That's fine.

Mrs. R: I could also model notes during sections of the lesson you and I plan for—so you will be a part of the process. We could also switch roles . . . where we alternate between who will share the information out loud and who will model note-taking. There are many options for us to consider. How about we meet tomorrow to figure this out?

Mr. B: Sounds good to me.

Mindfulness as a Solution

Mrs. R. clearly embraced the perspective of Mr. B—even though he was resistant and seemingly closed to new ideas. Mrs. R. invited new ways of doing things—invited change as an extension to what he was already doing. She did this in a way that guided change through the familiar. His perspective was still valued—yet extended thinking occurred as she steered him to view the situation within a co-teaching mindset.

Flexible Grouping

Flexible grouping is a strategy for differentiating instruction to allow students the opportunity to work together in various ways. Groupings may be whole group, small group, pairs, triads, etc. There will be times when teachers opt to include the choice for students to "go solo" if beneficial for the students and the specific activity. The groups may be teacher led or student led—depending on the activity, learning goals, and students' needs. Flexible groupings have great possibilities to increase student engagement, motivation, communication skills, and problem solving abilities. Marzano, Pickering, and Pollock (2001) shared the following guidelines for managing flexible grouping:

◆   Consider your learning goal—then decide which grouping structure would best apply.

◆ Create a class checklist to document student performance and learning outcomes to keep track of what works well. This data will inform future instructional decisions.

◆ Demonstrate the task through explicit instruction such as teacher modeling before groups begin to work to ensure everyone knows what to do; make goals and procedural steps clear.

◆ Be mindful of the time. do not give too much or too little time. Gauge the learning task with students' performance and adjust accordingly.

◆ Following the group work, return to whole class setting to share outcomes as a community of learners.

◆ Consider having students keep a learning log to reflect on their learning for the day. This could become a valuable formative assessment tool!

✅ Co-Teaching Connections

Select three to five ideas from this chapter and share how you may connect each with your co-teaching experience. How does it connect with what you are already doing? How could you extend and apply in your classroom? What could it look like? What would the students be doing? Describe the role of you and your co-teacher. Share your ideas with your co-teacher—and listen to his or her ideas as well—and let the co-teaching connections begin!

_____

_____

_____

_____

💡 Key Ideas

Critical thinking is a necessary component for teachers to consider as they design instruction.

Depths of Knowledge (DOK) framework offers opportunities for teachers to vary the levels of thinking they offer for deeper student learning, engagement, and achievement.

Co-teachers have many options for modeling strategies that encourage students to extend their thinking within the process of learning each day.

Bloom's Taxonomy, Maslow's hierarchy, Webb's Depths of Knowledge, and Costa and Kallick's habits of mind are important to consider as lessons are designed to deepen the
learning for all learners—including the two teachers in the room.

References

Anderson, L. W., Krathwohl, D. R., & Bloom, B. S. (2001). *A taxonomy for learning, teaching, and assessing: A revision of Bloom's taxonomy of educational objectives.* New York, NY: Longman.

Anderson, R. C., & Pearson, P. D. (1984). A schema-theoretic view of basic processes in reading comprehension. *Handbook of Reading Research, 1,* 255–291.

Bartlett, F. C. (1932). *Remembering: An experimental and social study.* Cambridge: Cambridge University Press.

Bloom, B., Englehart, M. Furst., Hill, W., & Krathwohl, D. (1956). *Taxonomy of educational objectives: The classification of educational goals. Handbook I: Cognitive domain.* New York, Toronto: Longmans, Green.

Bruner, J. S. (1979). *On knowing: Essays for the left hand.* Cambridge, MA: Harvard University Press.

Costa, A. L., & Kallick, B. (2000). *Discovering & exploring habits of mind. A developmental series, book 1.* Alexandria, VA: Association for Supervision and Curriculum Development.

Duron, R., Limbach, B., & Waugh, W. (2006). Critical thinking framework for any discipline. *International Journal of Teaching and Learning in Higher Education, 17*(2), 160–166.

Dwyer, C. P., Hogan, M. J., & Stewart, I. (2012). An evaluation of argument mapping as a method of enhancing critical thinking performance in e-learning environments. *Metacognition and Learning, 7*(3), 219–244.

Elder, L., & Paul, R. (1994). Critical thinking: Why we must transform our teaching. *Journal of Developmental Education, 18*(1), 34.

Harris, T. L., & Hodges, R. E. (1995). *The literacy dictionary: The vocabulary of reading and writing.* Newark, DE: International Reading Association.

Hattie, J. (2012). *Visible learning for teachers: Maximizing impact on learning.* New York, NY: Routledge.

Langer, E. J. (2014). *Mindfulness.* Boston, MA: Da Capo Press.

MacDonald, E., & Shirley, D. (2009). *The mindful teacher.* New York, NY: Teachers College Press.

Marin, L. M., & Halpern, D. F. (2011). Pedagogy for developing critical thinking in adolescents: Explicit instruction produces greatest gains. *Thinking Skills and Creativity, 6*(1), 1–13.

Marzano, R. J. (2004). *Building background knowledge for academic achievement: Research on what works in schools.* Alexandria, VA: Association for Supervision and Curriculum Development.

Marzano, R. J., Pickering, D. J., & Pollock, J. E. (2001). *Classroom instruction that works: Research-based strategies for increasing student achievement.* Alexandria, VA: Association for Supervision and Curriculum Development.

Maslow, A. H. (1943). A theory of human motivation. *Psychological Review, 50*(4), 370.

Norris, S. P. (1985). Synthesis of research on critical thinking. *Educational Leadership, 42*(8), 40–45.

Petress, K. (2004). Critical thinking: An extended definition. *Education, 124*(3), 461.

Piaget, J. & Inhelder, B. (1969). *The psychology of the child. New York: Basic Books.*

Rosen, Y., & Tager, M. (2014). Making student thinking visible through a concept map in computer-based assessment of critical thinking. *Journal of Educational Computing Research, 50*(2), 249–270.

Webb, N. L. (1997). *Determining alignment of expectations and assessments in mathematics and science education (National Institute for Science Education Brief, Vol. 1, No. 2).* Madison, WI: National Institute for Science Education, University of Wisconsin-Madison.

Webb, N. L. (2002). An analysis of the alignment between mathematics standards and assessments. A paper presented at the American Educational Research Association Annual Meeting, New Orleans, Louisiana April 1–5, 2002.

Wyse, A. E., & Viger, S. G. (2011). How item writers understand depth of knowledge. *Educational Assessment, 16*(4), 185–206.

3

Classroom Management: Co-Creating Meaningful Learning Environments

Essential Questions

1. What are the elements of classroom management—and how may co-teachers embed effective strategies to build a strong management foundation?
2. How can co-teachers co-create effective learning space and routines?
3. How could the process of restorative justice and application of mindfulness strategies empower learners?

Keep the work interesting and the discipline takes care of itself.

—E. B. White

It is often the case that co-teachers grapple with the "if mom says no, then let's ask dad" syndrome. Students may easily take advantage of the varying personalities and philosophies held by the two teachers in the room. Co-teachers, however, must unite! They must work together to co-create meaningful learning environments.

According to Gately and Gately (2001), classroom management involves two elements: structure and relationships. Structure involves the routines, rules, and procedures that guide the ins and outs of the flow of activities throughout the day. Relationships cultivate a respectful, compassionate, and inspiring learning environment that makes everyone *want* to be in the room—learning together. Positive relationships encourage the motivation to naturally and respectfully follow rules and procedures (Marzano, Marzano, & Pickering, 2003).

The teachers' belief systems play a vital role in creating the foundation for any classroom management system. Co-teachers must share in the basic practices of respect and belief that each student has the capacity to learn—and together they can optimize learning outcomes (Darch & Kame'enui, 2004). Darch and Kame'enui (2004) share three key principles to guide co-teachers to align their co-teaching mission:

1. Teachers play a profound role in how, what, and why students learn.
2. Teachers must create as many learning opportunities as possible.
3. Teachers guide students to build upon background knowledge and extend beyond their comfort zones toward new accomplishments.

Co-teachers must remember to treat students with respect; believe that each learner has a personal capacity to learn; and trust that each learner behaves in a way that is purposeful, strategic, and intelligent (Darch & Kame'enui, 2004). The principles shared above are meaningful for any teacher to follow—but just think of the power and potential of two teachers in the room! Friend and Cook (2007) claim that co-teachers should extend their core beliefs and philosophies and share in a collaborative design for managing academic and social behaviors. Co-teachers should begin by sharing their personal beliefs and then discussing classroom routines and what they believe constitutes appropriate student behavior. It's a conversation co-teachers must have in order to be proactive in designing the learning environment.

Tips for Co-Creating a Shared Learning Space

- ◆ **Plan for your plan:** Before meeting together to discuss, write down a few of your non-negotiable beliefs for a smooth-running classroom environment. What must happen for you as a teacher to instill a meaningful learning environment? Write down three to five firm personal beliefs.
- ◆ **Start with the big ideas:** What are the three to five broad expectations you have for the way students should behave? For example, two common expectations are that students will be respectful and responsible.
- ◆ **Be specific:** During the meeting time to discuss your classroom management ideas, make sure to be clear—make your thinking visible. For example, if co-teachers agree on responsibility as a must-include component of effective classroom management, then discuss what that really looks like. If a student forgets his homework or a pencil—how will that be handled? Will one co-teacher mind if the other co-teacher provides a pencil any time a student needs one? These minor, but potentially distracting, interferences must be openly discussed to avoid communication barriers along the way.
- ◆ **Put your ideas in writing:** One of you should take notes on the big ideas, questions, comments, concerns, and celebratory ideas shared during your

TABLE 3.1 Questions to Guide Co-Teaching Classroom Management Conversations

Need (According to Maslow's hierarchy)	Questions to guide discussions and action steps
Knowledge and Understanding	• What are the individual strengths and needs of our students? • What are some instructional approaches that could be implemented to guide student learning? • What specific methods and routines should be in place to support individual as well as whole class learning?
Belonging and Self-Esteem	• What will we do to guide our students' success? How will we cultivate a sense of community? • How will we foster student ownership and pride in their learning efforts and outcomes?
Safety and Security	• What will we do if a student is disruptive? What constitutes disruptive behaviors? How will we make sure we both interact with all students? What supports and scaffolds do we need to put in place to meet the needs of the individuals in our classroom?

time together. Make a copy for each teacher to refer to when needed. It can be a powerful way of building a co-teaching foundation with the aim of it becoming stronger as your experiences unfold.

◆ **Apply Maslow's hierarchy of needs** as a great place to start to guide you and your co-teacher to develop a comprehensive plan to create a comfortable, risk-free learning environment.

Use Table 3.1 as a guide your discussions to ensure you consider the needs of all students.

The following is a list of additional classroom management checkpoints for co-teachers to consider as they proactively set up for a successful year.

◆ Discuss how to set up the room: How will the desks be arranged?
◆ Discuss views on flexibility to arrange desks to encourage options for whole class, small groups, and student-pair work.
◆ How will parent communication be set up for successful ongoing communications with both teachers?
◆ What will the daily routine look like?
◆ What is each teacher's philosophy on grading?
◆ How will we set up the instructional structure to ensure both teachers play an active role? (Altering your use of the co-teaching models will take care of this!).
◆ Go slowly. Beginning with one co-teaching model to start—such as the parallel teaching model—will allow each of you to ease into your roles, while learning about one another.
◆ Make time to debrief. Make this part of your routine. Check in with one another to ensure that feelings are shared and disagreements become resolved in a timely manner. Making this part of your schedule also allows

for compliments and celebrations to occur frequently—furthering the co-teaching relationship with one another and with students.

◆ Consider co-creating "Classroom Beliefs" or a "Class Mission Statement" to encourage students to take part in the creation of what is acceptable behavior.

Once co-teachers have reached an agreement on creating an initial structure, they must design instruction in a way that embeds teaching students these classroom behaviors. MacDonald and Shirley (2009) identified The Triple Tensions that they believe express permanent dilemmas in any classroom that may interfere with instruction. The Triple Tensions (adapted from MacDonald & Shirley, 2009, p. 81) are:

1. **Contemplation and Action:** More time is often needed to think—just as individuals may often be inclined to respond impulsively. Just think about the students who love to call out! Or the students who need additional time to process their thoughts.

2. **Ethics and Power:** A person may become preoccupied with his or her own beliefs and therefore withdraw from the conversation or activity. In addition, a person may become overcome with power and inadvertently (or directly) disrupt the flow of a lesson. Think about those students who stay quiet—even though you sense they have a lot to say. Or the students— the same students—who constantly raise their hands or interrupt to get share their response—which may lead to intimidating others who want to contribute to the conversation or lesson activity.

3. **The Individual and the Collective:** There are always times when one individual needs to stand up with moral courage to pave the way for thinking and positive actions steps for the group. There are other times individuals need to compromise their own wishes to respectfully go along with the majority to uphold a democratic process.

As you read through the three tensions, did any students come to mind? Perhaps an experience between you and colleagues also resonated with you. Take a minute to write down your connections with The Triple Tensions. Do you agree these are permanent dilemmas in the teaching and learning process?

_____

_____

MacDonald and Shirley (2009) suggest using a Tuning Protocol (Blythe, Allen, & Powell, 1999) within small groups to guide teachers to regulate potential conflicts that could arise in the classroom as a result of The Triple Tensions. Implementing the following protocol could support co-creating a sense of community as students practice meaningful collaboration—while embedding critical thinking skills.

The Tuning Protocol Procedures

Step 1: Presentation (5–10 minutes) One student presents information with an emphasis on the learning that took place and concludes with a focus question with the aim of receiving feedback and assistance to deepen the learning. Presenter may share work samples and learning goals. Participants are silent during this presentation.

Step 2: Clarifying Questions (5 minutes) Group asks the presenter questions that clarify the information shared. Clarifying questions require a simple statement response—such as yes and no responses.

Step 3: Examination (10–15 minutes) Participants look closely at the work, taking notes on where it seems to be in tune with the stated goals along with where any questions arise. Participants specifically focus on examining the work in light of the presenter's focus question. Presenter is silent during this time. He or she listens to the group discussing what was presented.

Step 4: Pause to Reflect on Warm and Cool Feedback (5 minutes) Each participant silently reflects on what he or she will share with the presenter.

Step 5: Warm and Cool Feedback (10–15 minutes) Participants share feedback with each other while the presenter is silent. The discussion begins with some warm feedback in response to the presenter's focus question. The discussion evolves to cool, reflective feedback to provide the presenter with varying feedback with the aim of deepening the learning.

Step 6: Group Share: A discussion with the presenter and the participants may follow to conclude the learning process.

Classroom management includes teachers being keen observers of the outcomes of the daily instructional routines. It becomes evident that some students require additional scaffolds and supports. Co-teachers can naturally reinforce students' abilities to contribute to a positive learning environment by embedding supports throughout the day to keep students' attention and behavior in check. Lesson plans should include co-teaching structures that facilitate the acquisition of skills for students requiring more review. Visual cue cards listing rules and procedures can be made available to these students in addition to more frequent cueing, reinforcement, and opportunities for self-management. Guiding students to self-regulate their thoughts and actions can go a long way—and may be achieved through mindful activities to create autonomy and achievements.

Managing Behaviors

As discussed so far, classroom management involves the decisions teachers make to set up the physical routines and classroom structures. Another crucial element in the implementation of effective management skills involves students becoming aware of their thoughts that lead to their actions—and therefore—their consequences. Co-teachers may increase students' abilities to become a cooperative, collaborative part of the management process. It all begins with being accountable—and mindful. As discussed in Chapter 2, mindfulness techniques may contribute to creating positive relationships within any learning environment. The premise of mindfulness can be extended as we consider how it may connect with developing effective management skills.

Begin with a Bit of Student Mindfulness

Mindfulness is the process of being aware in order to be kind, curious, and nonjudgmental within the moments. It is an awareness and practice of being present in the moment (Srinivasan, 2014). When we are present in the moment, we become keenly aware of our own emotions in response to our surroundings. We know if we are feeling comfortable with the temperature in the room. We know how we are feeling—specifically, we know if we are upset, content, relaxed, or stressed. If we reflect upon our emotions, we may even be able to isolate the cause of the way we are feeling. In a classroom situation, we can all remember those teachers who created a risk-free, comfortable learning environment. Our emotional levels were in check—we felt a sense of belonging. Yet, school experiences easily overflow with mindlessness. Rather than being present in the moment, teachers and students alike partake in a status quo "let's just get through this" kind of attitude. Often they are really thinking about something that happened in the past—or worrying about something about to happen in the near future. Langer (1989) explored the implications of mindfulness and found that no matter what task we set out to accomplish, our mindsets—our attitude and belief systems—adversely affect our ability to learn. For example, a student who comes to class may take a seat as the bell rings and sit quietly, ready for class to begin—but mindlessly accepts the information that the teacher begins to share. This disengaged, "going through the motions" kind of experience results in an overflow of mindlessness in classrooms. Fortunately, there are simple ways of increasing mindfulness in learning.

Mindfulness activities allow for us to be responsive and engaged rather than reactive and detached from learning (Srinivasan, 2014). To encourage mindful students, we must become mindful teachers. Co-teachers may choose to engage in these peaceful moments together—or separately. Either way, co-teachers will find that, in time, they feel more responsive to the ideas of others—along with having a more clear and patient perspective when interacting with students and colleagues. These tips for teachers are also very effective quick exercises to use with students as well.

Three Quick Mindful Tips for Teachers

◆ **Observe your breath**—Take 3 minutes to just notice your breath—do not judge it—just follow your inhale and exhale—bring all your attention to following your breath. You will be surprised how clear your mind becomes—and how energized you feel. Whatever was worrying you will soon fade away . . . nothing but your breath matters—a sense of peaceful calm will be your focus. Your breath brings you to notice the power of possibilities in the present moment.

◆ **Set an intention**—Take 3–5 minutes to sit quietly and think about your intention for the day. If time, take a minute or two in between activities to reflect on your intention and adjust as necessary. This intention could do wonders to keep you focused on a clear, productive path throughout the day.

◆ **Listen to a mindfulness bell**—Mindfulness bells are easy to find, but any bell will do for this exercise to guide you to be in the present moment. Tap the bell and listen to the sound it makes as it vibrates—pay attention only to this sound as it fades. Continue to listen until the sound fades away completely. Notice how you feel. Repeat as often as you need within your given timeframe until you notice a sense of calm.

Tips for Positive Attention and Behavior Outcomes

Attention and emotions have been understood as central to learning as well as in mindfulness research (Langer, 1989). In her research, Langer found that when people were introduced to a variety of stimuli, as opposed to just being exposed to one stimulus, their memory improved. The implications for teaching indicate that mindful attention can result in improved memory and engagement (Langer & Moldoveanu, 2000).

Three Tips for Mindfulness With Students

1. **Incorporate Breath Work:** Breathing mindfully involves simply noticing your breath as you inhale and exhale. To guide students through the awareness, suggest they begin with saying "in—peace" as they inhale and "out—harmony" (or simply "in" and "out") making sure to guide them to take a deep breath in and a long exhale out. This breath work may be done at any point in the day. Co-teachers may weave this through transition times—and students may decide to quietly take a "breath break" as they individually need. You may also introduce a visual to the process by encouraging students to visualize the in-breath as one color and the out-breath as another. The possibilities to incorporate mindful breaths are endless—and will most certainly positively impact classroom management.

2. **Integrate Paying Attention**: Take 3–10 minutes to invite students to focus on one object or spot anywhere in the room. Their gaze should be fixed on this spot or object. Encourage students to keep track of their thoughts as they stare at this spot by placing a tally mark in the "past" box or the "future" box as they become aware of each thought.

TABLE 3.2 Tally Boxes for Paying Attention Exercise

Past	Future

Encourage students to:

◆ Notice how many times inner thoughts take them away from the present moment.
◆ Notice the breath—just pay attention to the in-breath and out-breath as they gaze at a spot or object in the room.
◆ Following the activity, ask students to either share out loud how the activity made them feel or ask them to write or sketch how they are feeling as a result of these peaceful moments. They should be all set to pay attention to the next lesson with greater focus!

Give this and all mindful activities some time before deciding if they work for you and your students. It takes time to step out of one's comfort zones to take notice of one's own breathing and feelings. It is not something people are used to doing— especially in schools. Students are creatures of the habit of mindlessness as they go through the predictable structure of the school day—they go through the motions, all too often, with less-than-enthusiastic compliancy. So be patient to give mindfulness a chance—you and your co-teacher will certainly reap the benefits of more responsive students throughout your daily routines as you co-create a harmonious, productive learning environment.

3. **Create Visual Anchor Chart**: Often, teachers post classroom rules as a way to foster positive attention and behaviors. Consider the classroom chart in Table 3.3 that could serve to illuminate mindfulness in your classroom.

TABLE 3.3 Sample Classroom Chart (adapted from Srinivasan, 2014, p. 184)

Benefits of Practicing Mindfulness
• I can strengthen my focus and attention to the present moment.
• I become aware and understanding of my emotions.
• Being present helps me to manage stress and anxiety.
• When I am mindful, I create a sense of inner calm and peace.
• Mindfulness promotes compassion and kindness with myself and others.
• I become resilient—I can push through challenges—and learn from mistakes.
• When I am mindful, my mind is clear and focused; therefore, I am a strong listener and speaker.
• Mindfulness creates a sense of clarity; therefore, I make effective decisions.

Classroom Management With Growth Mindset

Connecting Mindfulness to Learning: Inspire a Growth Mindset

Psychologist Carol Dweck (2006) tells us that some people embrace a fixed mindset, which results in the belief that their basic qualities or abilities cannot be developed or changed, so they are less motivated to work hard and learn. In contrast, those with a growth mindset believe that if they work hard, they can improve and increase their abilities. Effort is a key variable in embracing learning as a meaningful process—but effort alone is not enough. Dweck (2015) explains that students must be flexible in trying new ways of achieving their goals. The following tips and strategies can guide co-teachers to expand learning possibilities for students:

1. **Expand students' repertoire of strategies**: Students must be flexible thinkers and be willing to apply new strategies and seek resources that could help them to problem solve when they get stuck along the natural process of learning.
2. **Encourage short and long term positive effects**: Co-teachers can provide oral feedback, such as "So far, your abilities show . . . and . . . is a good place to continue working toward your goals." Teachers may also provide written feedback when commenting on assignments—such as the "I noticed—work on" specific feedback sheet.
3. **The Power of *Yet***: Dweck (2014) shared her passion for language and the power of adding the word *yet* when describing our abilities. For example, when someone says, *I'm not good at math*—it automatically provides a shut down, closed off, unreachable feeling. But look what happens when the word *yet* is added at the end of the sentence: *I am not good at math yet*. Oh, the empowerment—the possibilities—and the opportunities for self-motivation as one works towards improving. Our language can serve to empower one's actions to push through setbacks and challenges.

Mindfulness and growth mindset may become a natural foundation for positive classroom management in developing a learning environment where students learn to value their own thinking as well as the thinking of others along a meaningful process of learning. Something else to keep in mind when thinking about growth mindset is that everyone is a work in progress. We are all along a powerful process of becoming . . . and of growing. There will be times when a fixed mindset embodies our thoughts and actions—and that is to be expected. Teachers, however, have

TABLE 3.4 Specific Feedback Sheet

What I noticed you did well	What you may continue to work on

the extraordinary opportunity to gently shift students' beliefs about themselves as individuals—and as learners. If we can become mindful of the process—if we can encourage our students to become mindful of the process—a positive learning environment will be established in the classroom that encourages positive attitudes toward learning for each students' future.

Strategies shared throughout this book naturally embed approaches to nurture mindfulness and growth mindset within the instructional process, so co-teachers can do everything they can to unlock learning opportunities each day.

Classroom Management, Moral Identity, and Behaviors

What about those disruptive behaviors? What about students who just won't buy into shifting their thinking? For starters, if co-teachers really embrace mindfulness and model the positive effects of perseverance and resiliency along with a consistent message of care and compassion, students are apt to want to be in class—attentive—or at least open up and speak privately with a teacher who can be trusted. Students like to feel cared for—who doesn't, right? In constructing our moral identities as educators, Noddings (1984) can be especially compelling. Noddings presented an ideal professional practice grounded in caring for and with our students. When adhering to an ethics of caring, co-teachers should:

◆ Care for the well being of each other—and all students.
◆ Commit to helping each other (and all students) to grow and to achieve to one's personal best.
◆ Be receptive and responsive to the needs of each other—consider each other's feelings.
◆ Be aware of one's own perspective while considering another point of view.

Mindful Tools and Strategies for Effective Classroom Management

1. **Mindset Check-In:** Co-teachers may decide to provide time for students to check in with their attitudes towards learning. Inspired by the "Effective Effort Rubric" at Mindset Works (2014), I collaborated with colleague, Joshua Hendrickson, to develop a tool for students to begin to connect their thoughts with their attitudes about themselves as learners. We made sure to provide the opportunity for learners to feel the flow of the natural range of emotions individuals feel as they engage with the learning process (see student work sample in Figure 3.1).

This mindset check-in was applied during a transition between a math lesson and an English lesson. It was apparent that the student was frustrated during the lesson, so the student was given the choice to complete the check-in as a way to re-channel his thoughts and behaviors. It was so interesting how the student, when given the

Figure 3.1 Student Mindset Check-In Sample: Michael

Name *Michael*   Date *2/3*

The learning experience I will think about is:

Working on not giving up

For each of the rows below, mark a point on the line to show how you responded to the above situation. Then complete the statement on the right.

In the situation above I...		I know this because...
At times I felt overwhelmed and unmotivated	I embraced challenges and pushed through	*When I keep on working to continue*
At moments I felt like I wanted to give up	I persisted and applied myself through setbacks	*Lots of work*
Most of the time I put forth little effort	I put forth my best effort most of the time	*I make sure to take a break and go back to it*
Most of the time I ignored feedback from teachers or peers	I learned from feedback and it helped me to improve and push through challenges	*People showed me how I can keep trying*
At times I felt uncomfortable by the success of others	I was inspired by the success of others	*I like to listen to other people share their work*

Adapted by E. Stein in collaboration with J. Hendrickson 2015
Source: Mindset Works, Inc. 2002–2012

choice to reflect on the frustrating experience, reflected on the challenge in a positive way. He identified that asking for help from peers and teachers helped him to push through the challenge. In addition, he acknowledged that he was inspired by the success of others students; he figured if they could do it, so could he. See Figure 3.2 to see how another student decided to check-in with different results. Her reflections in the moments served to change her attitude and body language from a withdrawn, detached mode to a more relaxed manner as she accepted the challenge for the time being. She acknowledged that in the moments of that class, she just didn't care about the math lesson. With two teachers in the room, it was easy for one co-teacher to work with the students who opted to complete the check-in while the other teacher continued to support the learning for the math lesson.

The Mindset Check-In served to validate and shift these two students toward resiliency and a relaxed perspective toward their learning abilities. They went from feeling frustrated—and worried about an upcoming math test—to present in the moment with an acceptance and peaceful manner.

2. **Strategy Wall:** Create a chart to display what students can do if they are feeling stressed, overwhelmed, or frustrated. You could include:
   ◆ Visualize a calm, happy place.
   ◆ Talk to a teacher and/or a peer.
   ◆ Sketch your feelings on a sticky note or in a notebook.
   ◆ Think of one positive event or fact that is relevant to you.
   ◆ Take five deep breaths—(using breath work techniques shared earlier in this chapter).
   ◆ Listen to music.
   ◆ Look out the window and focus on what you notice in nature.
3. **Mood Meter:** The Yale Center for Emotional Intelligence (2014) created the mood meter as a self-awareness tool to guide self-regulation and better decision-making. Increasing one's vocabulary around expressing emotions is another benefit of the mood meter exercise.

What Is the Mood Meter?

The Mood Meter is a square divided into four quadrants: Each quadrant represents a different set of feelings and levels of energy (see page 57).

The top left quadrant (may be represented with the color red) indicates emotions such as angry, scared, and anxious.

The bottom left quadrant (may be represented with the color blue) indicates emotions such as sad, disappointed, and lonely.

The bottom right quadrant (may be represented with the color green) indicates peaceful, calm, tranquil, and relaxed emotions.

The top right quadrant (may be represented with the color yellow) indicates happy, excited, energized, eager, and curious emotions.

Figure 3.2 Student Mindset Check-In Sample: Vanessa

Mindset Check-in

Name *Vanessa*   Date *January 23rd 2015*

The learning experience I will think about is:

Learning Math

For each of the rows below, mark a point on the line to show how you responded to the above situation. Then complete the statement on the right.

In the situation above I...		I know this because...
At times I felt overwhelmed and unmotivated ×————————	I embraced challenges and pushed through	*I did not want to try*
At moments I felt like I wanted to give up ×————————	I persisted and applied myself through setbacks	*I felt like giving up*
Most of the time I put forth little effort ×————————	I put forth my best effort most of the time	*I did not want to do it*
Most of the time I ignored feedback from teachers or peers ×————————	I learned from feedback and it helped me to improve and push through challenges	*because I did not really care*
At times I felt uncomfortable by the success of others ————×————	I was inspired by the success of others	*I did not really care*

Adapted by E. Stein in collaboration with J. Hendrickson 2015
Source: Mindset Works, Inc. 2002–2012

Figure 3.3 Mood Meter

How to Use the Mood Meter

◆ Create a mood meter on a PowerPoint slide, large chart paper, and/or small individual student copies. You may decide to use the different colored quadrants or just use the quadrants on a single colored paper with each quadrant labeled with descriptive feeling words.

◆ Encourage students to plot their feelings several times throughout the day or week to track their emotions and how they connect with their decisions and actions.

◆ Teachers may use this as a tool to encourage communication. For example, using the tool as a visual, students could express how they are feeling. In addition, teachers may initiate a conversation, if needed, for example, "I see you seem in the red right now—what can I do to help you?"

Like mindfulness and growth mindset, and anything worthwhile, developing emotional self-awareness takes time, patience, and practice. Over time, the Mood Meter can become an intuitive, powerful tool for students to feel validated, safe, and understood. It could be a proactive tool in diminishing disruptive classroom behaviors, deepening a sense of emotional self-awareness, and building better relationships for a successful learning environment.

4. **Classroom Management Through a Restorative Justice Approach**

Typically, classroom management involves a system for handling behaviors that is consistent with punitive approaches where there is a negative consequence for specific behaviors. At the elementary levels, a visit to the principal's office is equated with a student who needs to be reprimanded with the decision to separate him or her from the class. At the secondary levels, there is typically a zero tolerance policy, which consists of in- or out-of-school suspensions that are put into place with the intent to shape and manage student behaviors. At the classroom levels, teachers put point systems or a three-strikes-you-are-out approach to guiding students to follow routines in an appropriate manner. Typically, when students are separated from the group, the threat of consequences (such as a trip to the principal's office, an in-school suspension, or earning or losing a point in the class point system) poses a threat to the student(s) and undermines relationships. The locus of control is on the adult—and an air of anxiety is created. Democratic approaches where students have a bit more freedom and voice in the process of managing behaviors conflict with current discipline practices (Evans & Lester, 2010). Research shares the need for alternate approaches to classroom and discipline. Extensive research has shown a zero tolerance policy to be ineffective at best (Anfara, Evans, & Lester, 2013). Evans and Lester (2010) claimed a restorative justice approach could be exactly what schools need in order to meaningfully shape and direct student behaviors.

What Is Restorative Justice?

The premise of restorative justice in classrooms is to build community and to manage challenging behaviors to create a meaningful learning environment. Restorative justice serves as a pedagogical process as well as a conflict resolution approach that invites students to be a part of co-creating a safe and productive learning community. Restorative justice methodologies create a safe space and structure to build an inclusive community through an organic process that is built upon relationships between teachers and students—as well as on students' peer interactions. A restorative justice approach also provides authentic educational modeling of effective social and communication skills through a collective problem solving process. Students have the opportunity to reflect on learning behaviors through collective conferencing methods that involve teachers and students sharing their feelings and perspectives on a given situation. (Rinker & Jonason, 2014). Cameron and Thorsborne (2001) claimed that through the lens of restorative justice, misconduct is not viewed as a rule-breaking action against a school policy, but rather as a violation against people and relationships. Misbehaviors are not reacted to with punitive, isolated experiences—but they are responded to with compassionate, collaborative efforts by all involved.

Principles of Restorative Justice (Anfara, Evans, & Lester, 2013)

1. **Meet Student Needs:** View student behavior as a form of communication. What purpose does the behavior serve?
2. **Provide Accountability and Support:** Guide students to take responsibility for their actions and provide solutions (such as the strategies shared in this chapter) to scaffold their ability to independently self-regulate.
3. **Make Things Right:** Provide the opportunities for emotions to be shared. How do the students in the class feel about another student's misconduct? What solutions could be put in place for everyone to work as a team to support and care for one another?

4. **View the Conflict as a Learning Community**: Create open dialogues· and specific scaffolds to support the feeling of safety and compassion, so everyone is emotionally available to learn.

5. **Build Healthy Learning Communities:** Restorative justice is a way to respond to problematic behaviors—but it is also a proactive approach. Apply the principles of a safe, positive learning community as a way of preventing misconduct as well.

6. **Restore Relationships:** Work with and for students—as opposed to them feeling as though rules and procedures are happening to them or at them. Ensure that each student feels valued—that his or her perspective and feelings matter within a cycle of reciprocity—where each student is open to the perspectives and feelings of others.

7. **Address Power Imbalances:** Be sure to have students feel a part of the process of knowing their thoughts and actions are connected with the consequences of their decision to act a certain way. Balance the structure and authority with the space to allow students to take charge of their own learning and behaviors.

Restorative Justice in Action

Adopting a restorative justice approach involves a shift from punishment-oriented thinking to a process that involves restorative attitudes that create the space for productive dialogue to occur. Teachers and students practice the awareness and acceptance that all behaviors are a form of communicating. When a student is behaving in an undesirable manner, space is created for the teachers and classmates to accept, understand, and redirect with compassion. One key to applying restorative justice in a classroom is to be proactive through making time for students to reflect on how they are feeling—while making sure to include why they are experiencing a certain emotion. Within a co-taught classroom, two teachers have options for embracing this approach to managing student behaviors. The following restorative justice strategies promote self-reflection as students learn to proactively self-monitor their learning behaviors.

Restorative Justice Classroom Strategies

1. **Check-In:** Teachers may begin and end each day with a quick check-in sitting in a circle with students. They may choose for one person to begin and then go in order around the circle as each person shares one word (or one phrase) to describe how they are feeling at the current moment. Or each person may share their thoughts randomly as students chime in within the pragmatics of listening and sharing in a flexible process of compassion. As one person shares, everyone listens without asking any questions or elaborating. One co-teacher may select to take notes to notice themes within student responses over time. The notes could be used to initiate

necessary conversations in the future. At the end of the day teachers take a few minutes to again have students check-in with how they are feeling in general after a full school day—or they may reflect on a specific question, goal, or intention they set at the start of the day.

2. **Setting an Intention:** Setting a goal or intention at the start of each day can guide students to stay focused and push through challenges as they remain motivated to work toward their daily intention.

3. **Acceptance Circle:** Dialogue circles can be a powerful way to strengthen a sense of community when a student or students misbehave. For example, when a student constantly calls out or disrupts the learning process, this may be the perfect reason to find some time for a quick group conversation. Teachers and students sit in a circle to build an understanding and begin to create solutions around specific student behaviors—or a general issue needed to be solved within the classroom environment. This dialogue may unfold as a whole class experience, or one co-teacher may facilitate the dialogue with some students as the other teacher facilitates learning on another academic content area topic. After a designated amount of time, students may rotate activities so all students experience both learning groups. These restorative justice dialogues bring students' emotions to the forefront. Those students who feel that another's behavior has adversely affected them have a chance to discuss within a nurturing environment. The student(s) who displays undesirable behaviors has the opportunity to consider how his actions adversely affected others. It is helpful to clearly state the consequences of students' choices—acknowledging that they have the power to choose their own behavior. Encourage them to choose wisely. The consequences of their behaviors should be posed in a manner that empowers effective decisions. The next step is to brainstorm solutions for alternatives in student behaviors. The result of these dialogues can truly be meaningful justice for all involved.

4. **Revisit the Co-Teaching Models:** Teachers may wonder how they will have the time for restorative justice dialogues. With two teachers in the room, scheduling can be creative in support of making the time for students to self-regulate and be a part of this powerful learning community. Revisit the co-teaching models from Chapter 1 to proactively plan your plans for naturally embedding restorative justice in your classroom routines.

5. **Journaling:** Provide students with a notebook for them to document their feelings and provide class time to create entries. Teachers may have specific times during the day—or students may be invited to create entries whenever they need to quietly express their feelings to guide positive decisions and behaviors. Consider providing students with resources for expressing emotions—emojiis, words, or illustrations that help them to expand their emotional vocabulary and increase their ability to effectively communicate.

The following behavior management techniques have been influenced by Redl and Wineman (1952) and have been adapted here to share options for effective ways to de-escalate problematic behaviors—while guiding teachers to manage and promote successful learning behaviors and meaningful connections within a positive learning community.

1. *Proximity Control*: Co-teachers may take turns applying proximity to the student in the moments of a stressful situation to provide the student with additional support and a source of strength to push through any challenge.
2. *Planned Ignoring*: This technique involves the purposeful ignoring of a specific behavior as long as safety is not an issue. This is a good strategy to use if the teachers suspect the behavior is used to test the teachers. Ignoring the behavior shows our disapproval of that behavior—and therefore, does not provide unnecessary attention toward feeding into the unwanted behaviors. Once the behavior has passed, teachers may include the student into the activity to support his attention to the task.
3. *Signal Interference*: Create a signal with the student, such as a nod, thumbs up, or gesture to guide the student to self-monitor his behaviors. Signals are effective when used as a proactive tool to keep the student on track before troubling behaviors arise.
4. *Humor*: Laughter and humor can serve to alleviate unnecessary anxiety within the group. Teachers need to be mindful of when humor would be effective and when another tactic would be better. Humor can also serve to divert and redirect students, rather than paying direct attention to students' behavior, when it is wise to redirect with a potentially powerful refocusing tactic.
5. *Hurdle Help*: Teachers should be aware of when students are misbehaving due to an inability to cope with some aspect of the work. Notice the occasions when an instructional scaffold or some kind of assistance could redirect—or, better yet, proactively prevent—misconduct.
6. *Safe Space*: Have a space in the classroom where students can go to just take a quick break to regroup if they notice they are feeling stressed. Keep colored pencils and paper ready as a release for students to sketch or illustrate their thoughts and feelings. Keep a chart to guide emotion vocabulary words as they express their feelings on paper—in writing and/ or through drawing. Some students may just prefer to select a color to represent their mood—and just draw.
7. *Emotional Share Out*: Provide time for students to verbalize their stress, frustration, or anxiety as a means to positively direct the student to manage his emotions—rather than act out because that seems the only outlet. Providing this time gets students in the habit of meaningfully communicating their feelings in a socially appropriate manner. This may be done privately with one co-teacher and the student—or co-teachers may include this within the activity Acceptance Circle described on page 60.

8. *Post Clear Goals, Schedules, and Routines*: Sometimes students misbehave based on anxiety caused by the uncertainty of not knowing what is expected of them. Establish clear, consistent routines—while teaching students to be flexible through your open communication and modeling that sometimes routines need to be altered.

9. *Direct Appeal*: A direct verbal appeal to the student to discontinue the misbehavior may be sufficient to alter the situation. Be mindful to use this technique sparingly so students do not feel singled out. Clearly state the unacceptable behavior with clear direction for what the student should be doing. Students should feel the power of choice to behave accordingly and be responsible for the consequences of his or her choices.

10. *Encourage Rather Than Criticize*: Catch students doing something good! Positive reinforcement works wonders as well as specific feedback. "I noticed you helped Joey work through that math problem successfully!" "Your choice to let Stephanie go ahead of you in line was a thoughtful decision!" Encourage students by giving concrete, specific feedback and examples of their social, behavioral, and academic positive actions.

11. *No*: A strong, but thoughtful "no" provides the boundaries needed and welcomed by the students when appropriate—even if they do not realize it at the time. Stay strong, consistent, and compassionate. There are just those times when students need adult limits set.

12. *Life Space Interview (LSI)*: The following steps have been adapted from Redl et al. (1959). A life-space interview is perfect for that disruptive behavior that has occurred without any notice—behavior that needs direct intervention with the student's input in the solution-seeking process for redirecting the behaviors. The LSI must occur directly following the misbehavior. To optimize student's accountability and memory of the events of a situation, timing is everything for this technique to be effective.

How Does the Life Space Interview Work?

Step One: Isolate: The teacher and the student sit in a private space where they can dialogue to explore the student's point of view of the situation.

Step Two: Conversation Through Interview: The teacher asks the student to summarize the events of the situation that just occurred. The teacher facilitates the conversation to guide the student to connect the behaviors with feelings.

Step Three: Alternatives: The teacher guides the discussion by questioning the student for his or her suggestions for what he or she could do next time.

Step Four: Plan: Brainstorm, co-create, and discuss a plan of action.

Step Five: Practice: Student reenters class and has the opportunity to apply the plan of action—noticing the positive effects of his redirected behavioral choices and actions.

☑ Co-Teaching Connections

Select three to five ideas from this chapter and share how you may connect each with your co-teaching experience. How does it connect with what you are already doing? How could you extend and apply in your classroom? What could it look like? What would the students be doing? Describe the role of you and your co-teacher. Share your ideas with your co-teacher—and listen to his or her ideas as well—and let the co-teaching connections begin!

_____

_____

_____

_____

☼ Key Ideas

Classroom management is much more than setting up routines and procedures.

Classroom management can set the tone for a positive and productive learning environment for all learners.

Co-teachers can apply a variety of strategies to make students a part of co-creating positive learning environments.

A restorative justice approach can create a powerful process where students learn to take risks, strengthen self-regulation skills, and become a part of a meaningful learning classroom community.

Specific structures and strategies may be easily embedded within the instructional process, so managing student behaviors become closely linked and naturally aligned with an academic and social learning process.

When teachers embrace and apply a mindful, restorative approach, students have the opportunity to learn how to take charge of their thoughts and actions to make effective decisions within the moments of class time—and across time and settings.

References

Anfara, V. A., Jr., Evans, K. R., & Lester, J. N. (2013). Restorative justice in education: What we know so far. _Middle School Journal, 44_(5), 57–63.

Blythe, T., Allen, D., & Powell, B. S. (1999). _Looking together at student work: A companion guide to assessing student learning._ New York, NY: Teachers College Press.

Cameron, L., & Thorsborne, M. (2001). Restorative justice and school discipline: Mutually exclusive? In J. Braithwaite & H. Strang (Eds.), _Restorative justice and civil society_ (pp. 180–194). Cambridge, MA: Cambridge University Press.

Darch, C. B., & Kame'enui, E. J. (2004). *Instructional classroom management.* (2nd ed.). Upper Saddle River, NJ: Pearson Education.

Dweck, C. (2006). *Mindset: The new psychology of success.* New York, NY: Random House.

Dweck, C. (2014). The power of yet, TedxTalks. Retrieved from www.youtube.com/watch?v=J-swZaKN2lc

Dweck, C. (2015). Carol Dweck revisits the 'growth mindset'. *Education Week.*

Evans, K., & Lester, J. (2010). Classroom management and discipline: Responding to the needs of young adolescents. *Middle School Journal, 41*(3), 56–63.

Friend, M., & Cook, L. (2007). *Interactions: Collaboration skills for school professionals.* (5th ed.). Boston, MA: Allyn and Bacon.

Gately, S. E., & Gately, F. J. (2001). Understanding coteaching components. *Teaching Exceptional Children, 33*(4), 40–47.

Langer, E. J. (1989). *Mindfulness.* Reading, MA: Addison-Wesley/Addison Wesley Longman.

Langer, E. J., & Moldoveanu, M. (2000). The construct of mindfulness. *Journal of Social Issues, 56*(1), 1–9.

MacDonald, E., & Shirley, D. (2009). *The mindful teacher.* New York, NY: Teachers College Press.

Marzano, R., Marzano, J., & Pickering, D. (2003). *Classroom management that works: Research-based strategies for every teacher.* Alexandria, VA: Association for Supervision and Curriculum Development.

Mindset Works (2014). Effective effort rubric. Retrieved from www.mindsetworks.com/FileCenter/3JIQAYABR8M8GHQCQ05Q.pdf

Noddings, N. (1984). *Caring: A feminine approach to ethics and moral education.* Berkeley, CA: University of California Press.

Redl, F., Eveoleen, N., & Rexford, M. D. (1959). The life space interview workshop, 1957: Strategy techniques of the life space interview. *American Journal of Orthopsychiatry, 29*(1), 1–18. Doi: 10.1111/j.1939–0025.1959.tb00163.x

Redl, F., & Wineman, D. (1952). Controls from within: Techniques for the treatment of the aggressive child. *The American Journal of Nursing, 52*(10), 1281.

Rinker, J. A., & Jonason, C. (2014). Restorative justice as reflective practice and applied pedagogy on college campuses. *Journal of Peace Education, 11*(2), 162–180.

Srinivasan, M. (2014). *Teach, breathe, learn: Mindfulness in and out of the classroom.* Berkeley, CA: Parallax Press.

The Yale Center for Emotional Intelligence (2014). Mood Meter. Retrieved from http://ei.yale.edu/mood-meter-overview/

4

Setting the Stage for Self-Motivated Learners: Strategies for Motivation

Essential Questions

1. How can Pedagogical Content Knowledge empower a co-teaching relationship?
2. How can co-teachers transfer Ownership of Motivation with students?
3. What role does perception serve in motivation?
4. How does the belief in learner variability help to embrace the unique motivational profiles of students?
5. How may mind mapping be used as an exercise for supporting self-motivated learners?

A Multi-Dimensional View of Teacher Knowledge

One of the benefits to co-teaching is there are two teachers in the room. Two teachers with unique sets of skills and knowledge bases—two teachers who have so much to learn from one another. Without question, a strong knowledge base and breadth of content knowledge is a necessary requirement and goal of the learning process and outcomes of education. A well-developed foundation of subject knowledge is a necessary prerequisite for teaching effectively. Lambert (2009) claimed that in order for students to know how to think, they must have accurate knowledge to think about. Content-specific classroom teachers at the secondary levels are immersed in their content as the bell keeps ringing to dismiss and welcome groups of students to gain the knowledge they need to succeed in school. Primary teachers at the elementary levels have the challenging task of teaching all content area subjects, which results in varying degrees of success due to possible insufficient subject-specific training (Ofsted, 2011). Shulman (1986) posits that effective teachers—at any grade level—must possess Pedagogical Content Knowledge (PCK)—which he deems to be the necessary combined knowledge, skills, and attitude to teach any subject.

What Is Pedagogical Content Knowledge (PCK)?

According to Shulman (1987), PCK is all about making the subject matter comprehensible and accessible to others through a well-crafted blend and execution of a layered knowledge approach—specifically seven categories of teacher knowledge adapted here:

1. **General Pedagogical Knowledge:** Teachers have an understanding of broad principles and strategies for effective classroom management that set the foundation for learning to happen. General pedagogical knowledge has the potential to empower and transcend learning the subject matter beyond the moments of one specific class—or one particular academic test.

2. **Knowledge of Learners:** Understanding what makes learning this subject accessible or challenging. Grasping the knowledge that students of different abilities that students bring to any learning experience. Understanding individual learning characteristics and interests of the specific group of students in front of you is critical in sparking learning (see Student Profile Sheet in Appendix 2).

3. **Knowledge of Educational Contexts:** Understanding the intricacies of effective flexible groups, including whole class, small group, or individual processing time (See "Flexible Grouping" in Chapter 1). Knowledge of context may also include understanding the context of the subject and how you can guide students to connect to what they already know, so they can meaningfully build upon prior knowledge. (See Chapter 2 for strategies for activating schema.)

4. **Knowledge of Outcomes, Purpose, and Values:** Teachers need to have a clear sense of vision for the desired learning outcomes as well as the enthusiasm for engaging in the motivation to learn.

5. **Content Knowledge:** Teachers possess a sound knowledge base for the subjects they teach.

6. **Curriculum Knowledge:** Teachers embrace the materials and strategies and tap into these resources as effective tools that apply to specific lessons.

7. **Pedagogical Content Knowledge:** Understanding a variety of ways to represent the material in ways that guide learners to connect and construct meaning. This layer of knowledge includes the personal qualities that each teacher brings to his or her students.

The layers of knowledge needed to teach effectively go beyond just teaching the content. Schulman's theory of Pedagogical Content Knowledge guides us to see that the general knowledge needed to teach a subject is multidimensional. Specifically, the teacher's understanding of the content forms a solid foundation along a multi-faceted process for students to gain the knowledge and skills needed to connect with the learning in meaningful, long-lasting ways.

Pedagogical Content Knowledge and Student Motivation

We can use Shulman's PCK as a conceptual framework as we consider options for designing instruction that truly motivate and engage all students. Let's simplify this multi-layered process of knowledge with four guiding questions: *What is it I am teaching*? *How will I teach it*? *Why will I teach it this way*? and *How will I know when I have taught it*? Let's pause for a second. Consider how these four questions bring Schulman's categories of teachers' knowledge into manageable and meaningful action steps through the lesson design phase. We are reminded that what we teach is important—but the how and the why we teach is what really brings our lessons to life! Take a minute here to reflect on how you may change the way you design your instruction based on what you have read so far. How could Schulman's framework and the four guiding questions serve to direct you and your co-teacher to engage and motivate all of your students?

Bandura (2005) claimed another factor for strengthening motivation and student engagement lies in students' beliefs about themselves, their environment, and how their abilities fit with what is required of them in order to complete the task. Dweck and Leggett (1988) described motivated students as learners who seek challenging tasks and self-regulate effectively while working on these tasks. Motivated students demonstrate resilience through setbacks, and they exert more effort to find new ways of problem solving. Lin-Siegler, Dweck, and Cohen (2016) suggested educators could shape students' beliefs in ways that could positively impact their motivation, performance, and therefore their learning outcomes.

Strategies to Support Motivation and Engagement Through Pedagogical Content Knowledge (PCK)

Analogies
An analogy shows how two different things are similar by sharing a logical argument. The presenter of an analogy will often demonstrate how two things are alike by

pointing out shared characteristics—with the goal of showing that if two things are similar in some ways, they are similar in other ways as well. Wormeli (2009) considered analogies as power tools that could serve to guide students to connect a concrete idea to an abstract one. The Teach with Analogies (TWA) strategy (Glynn, Duit, & Thiele, 1995) applies shared attributes between a familiar concept (the analogue) and an unfamiliar one (the target) to guide students to create a mind map to relate the two ideas.

How an Analogy Works

1. Introduce the target concept.
2. Review the analogue concept.
3. Highlight relevant features of the target and the analogue.
4. Map the similarities.
5. Share the limitations of the analogy.
6. Draw a conclusion.

Example:

Analogy: Writing an essay is like playing a video game.

Introduce target concept: Writing an essay takes strategic thinking, patience, and concentration.

Review analogue concept: Playing a video game.

This should be a familiar concept. Even if a student doesn't play video games, he or she knows someone who does and is familiar with the concept.

Bring It Together: Identify Relevant Features of Target and Analogue

◆ Requires a step-by-step approach to learning.
◆ Others may model or demonstrate how to do it on your own.
◆ Takes concentration.
◆ Focus on the main theme, idea, or purpose.
◆ Create an outcome by following the steps and directions.

Map Similarities

Specify how each relevant feature is similar. Sketch it out—write it out—talk it out. Guide students to connect with the target concept through relating to a familiar concept.

Indicate the Limitations of the Analogy

Some students may have no experience with playing a video game.

The skill of writing is more complex, with modeling, support and practice needed throughout the writing process.

Writing is a needed skill to communicate—not just a skill for leisure.

Draw a Conclusion

The students develop a basic understanding of the writing process with the analogy of the process of how to play a video game.

Predict, Explain, Observe, & Explain (Palmer, 1996)

1. Students predict what will happen before reading, estimate the mathematical solution, or predict before participating in an experiment.
2. Students explain their prediction by justifying their thinking through sharing their reasons.
3. Students observe what happens as they read or work through a math problem or science experiment.
4. Students explain their observations.

Teacher Facilitated Discussions

Teachers lead the way to model enthusiasm and passion for learning. With a solid foundation of content knowledge, teachers weave in level questions (see Bloom's Taxonomy and Depths of Knowledge (DOK) from Chapter 2 to deepen the level of understanding within an engaging conversation.

Formative Assessments (Fisher & Frey, 2007)

Incorporate meaningful informal assessment tools that will engage and motivate students as they feel a sense of success within the moments of instruction. The completion of these informal assessments provides valuable information for teachers to assess what students have learned. When applying a Universal Design for Learning (UDL) lens (see Chapter 1), assessment is a natural, ongoing part of the learning process. Teachers should be checking for students' understanding by monitoring and measuring their performance of both the product and the process. Students are an active part of monitoring their own progress through opportunities to reflect on their performance (Meyer, Rose, and Gordon, 2014). If you review the strategies shared throughout this book, you will find some great examples of formative assessment possibilities. The following are few additional strategies to make time for as you assess your students' understanding within the actual moments of learning.

Cooperative Group Work (Johnson & Johnson, 2009)

Cooperative learning involves creating effective working relationships by setting goals with each member of the group taking an active role in the process of learning. The focus is on accomplishing a task through teamwork, peer support, collaboration, and effective communication skills. Having students work with peers is a powerful way to guide them to deepen their learning and extend their thinking. The following strategies support examples of cooperative learning.

Every Student Responds (ESR) Strategies (Himmele & Himmele, 2011)

ESR strategies keep all students actively engaged and motivated—simply by the teachers making time for valuing each voice in the room.

- ◆ *Rolling Discussions*—Encourage a conversation to move between teachers and students by holding a ball and initiating a conversation. The person who begins the conversation passes (tosses or rolls) the ball to someone in the group (great to arrange seats in a circle—or along the perimeter of the classroom). As the ball is passed each person who receives the ball adds to the conversation. Allow students to become leaders of the conversation to increase comfort, engagement, and motivation. This technique breaks the silence of many students who sit quietly as dominant hand-raisers typically take charge. This activity levels the playing field. Make it clear that the person with the ball must contribute something—it could be a summary statement to paraphrase what someone else said, it could be a question, or a connected thought. Keep it relaxed with a clear message—there are no right or wrong answers—only evolving thoughts!

◆ *Carousel Brainstorming*—The class forms groups of four to five students each. Each group gets their own chart and colored marker, so they can write down what they know about a given topic or they write possible answers to an open-ended question. Place a time limit for each group, and when the time is up have each group pass their chart along to another group—or you could have the students move to the next chart—movement is always a good idea to keep students engaged. Students must read what the other groups have recorded for answers and then add to the list. They can also add their voice to each group's chart as they review—they could underline, highlight, or write a comment or question for the creators of the chart to see once the carousel activity is completed.

◆ *Exit Tickets*—Provide students with an intriguing question, a math problem, a quote, or some other open-ended prompt to express their ability to perform a certain task, remember specific content, or review key vocabulary and main ideas. Exit tickets are often used as entrance tickets (as a warm-up activator!) with the same intent of gauging students' understanding and abilities—while activating their background knowledge, extending their thinking, and engaging them along a valuable learning process. Typically, students respond in writing—but this is a perfect opportunity to embed multiple means of action and expression (keeping UDL in mind from Chapter 1) and provide options for students to sketch their response or respond through oral communication.

◆ *Say Something*—Students form partners and simultaneously read a section of a text silently or one reads and the other student listens (remember to embed those UDL options whenever possible—this is a good example of providing multiple means of engagement, representation, and action and expression). When finished, they look away from the text and each student shares one fact or idea he or she remembers. This is great for strengthening working memory as students determine the important facts to remember. Remember to send a clear message—there are no right or wrong answers—only evolving thoughts! Students continue to read each section and pause for each partner to say something—it could be a key idea, concept, statement, connection, example to extend a thought—or a question. The process continues until the entire text is read. You may also apply Say Something on those days that you feel you and your co-teacher must present more lecture-style information—break it up with an engaging round of Say Something! This time you could break the lecture up with pairs sharing—with the option of a few reporting out to the class.

◆ *Roundtable*—Students from groups of five to six. (You could also apply this strategy whole class if you prefer.) One of the teachers shares a question or thinking prompt. Once students write their responses, they wait for the signal to pass their paper to the person to their right—or behind them. Now that students have a new response card, they add their voice to it—by writing (or sketching—remember UDL). Students keep passing papers within their group as teachers signal. At the end of the activity, students have not only deepened their perspective and knowledge, but they have also gained the perspective of their peers— where each voice is valued!

◆ *Response Cards*—This strategy is quick and simple—and works well with whole class or groups. One of the teachers asks a question or shares a prompt. Students respond by holding up a preprinted response card—for example, yes/no, true/false, agree/disagree—or of course you may use individual dry-erase boards for open-ended free-thinking responses.

How Can Co-Teachers Apply Pedagogical Content Knowledge (PCK) to Ramp Up Co-Teaching?

Step 1: Reflect: Each co-teacher embraces the concept of PCK and asks: *How do I connect and demonstrate this multi-dimensional view of the knowledge and skills needed to effectively teach?* Write your ideas down or just connect with your thoughts and be ready to share.

Step 2: Share your view of how you connect with PCK—What are your strengths? What skills do you feel you need to work on? Be ready to listen to your co-teacher's view of himself or herself.

Step 3: Compare, contrast, and apply. How are you and your co-teacher alike according to the PCK knowledge categories? How do you differ? How can you maximize your differences into actionable steps into the classroom? Which category of knowledge reveals a unique area(s) of expertise that each co-teacher bring to the learning each day?

Step 4: Review PCK implementation: Revisit discussions with your co-teacher. Set up a PCK debrief meeting once a week, once a month . . . or simply check in with each other through email or a shared Google Document to keep the multi-dimensional levels of knowledge flowing within your learning experiences. This step is necessary to keep the potential of the PCK framework naturally empowering your teaching skills as well as strengthening your relationships with your co-teacher, your students, and with the learning process itself!

Transferring Ownership of Motivation to Learners

For too long, in too many classrooms, students have come to class and waited for the teacher to begin the process of learning. You know what I mean—picture this: Students come to class, sit down (some even slouch), and they passively wait for class to begin—for learning to happen to them—for the bell to ring—or the lesson to just be over. They take in the information because they have learned to be obedient and compliant in the moments. It's been an issue teachers contend with for decades now. And it just doesn't make sense. Let's stand up—be the change that makes the difference—to guide students to shift from students waiting for teachers to entertain and enlighten to learners who inquire, seek, and thirst for knowledge in ways that make them responsible for their own learning. This does not have to just sound like a pipe dream or a segment from Mary Poppins—this is a very manageable and doable feat!

Shifting From Passive Students to Active Learners

Remember the question is: *How can we guide students to take charge of their learning process?* Let's immerse our attention in the ideas of motivation. How can teachers guide students to be self-motivated? The answer does not come without some work of our own to do—we must remember that we can do so much to facilitate this shift to happen. And with two teachers in the room—the possibilities are doubled!

Perception Drives Motivation

One very basic and deeply essential question teachers must ask is: *How am I presenting the information?* Is there a balance of auditory, visual, and kinesthetic options? I mean come on—if you are just talking to the class (notice that I said "talking to") and slapping up a PowerPoint slide to satisfy the need for visuals then it's no wonder you will have more students zoned out than in.

But if you incorporate strategies that invite meaningful participation and speak with students (notice the feel for the difference between *talking to* and *speaking with* students!), you will open many doors toward self-motivated learners. Let's begin with your decisions for presenting the content.

According to Meyer, Rose, and Gordon (2014) and the recognition principle (CAST, 2011), educators must provide multiple means of representation. As teachers plan for the "what" of learning, they consider how they plan for what the students will be *doing* as they gather facts, and categorize what is seen, and heard, and read. The UDL Guidelines can be a powerful tool for guiding teachers to remember that they must consider the variability that exists among all students. Learning happens within the context of the moments, and teachers must consider presenting information in a variety of ways. So keep a copy of the UDL Guidelines in your plan books and hang a copy on the wall—frame it—laminate it—and over

Figure 4.1 Representation Network with Connected Checkpoints
CAST (2011)

Provide Multiple Means of
Representation
Resourceful, knowledgeable learners

Provide options for comprehension
+ Activate or supply background knowledge
+ Highlight patterns, critical features, big ideas, and relationships
+ Guide information processing, visualization, and manipulation
+ Maximize transfer and generalization

Provide options for language, mathematical
expressions, and symbols
+ Clarify vocabulary and symbols
+ Clarity syntax and structure
+ Support decoding text, mathematical notation, and symbols
+ Promote understanding across languages
+ Illustrate through multiple media

Provide options for perception
+ Offer ways of customizing the display of information
+ Offer alternatives for auditory information
+ Offer alternatives for visual information

time you will naturally embrace and apply with ease. Notice the considerations for providing options for perception, language, and comprehension to guide instructional planning to address the natural varying abilities in our classrooms. Using the checkpoints as a guide, teachers weave in alternatives for students to perceive information. For example, they provide options for students to view images, words, multi-media video clips. They provide options for language by clarifying academic vocabulary and mathematical symbols. They provide options for comprehension through activating schema (discussed in Chapter 2) and guiding students to comprehend information through supports, such as providing additional processing time through peer interactions and strategies like the Three-Minute Pause strategy (discussed in this chapter).

Lavoie (2004) shared an important view of motivation in his mind-shifting F.A.T. City Workshop where he guided a group of participants to feel what it was like to go through school like a child with learning disabilities. As with all good practice, the insights, tips and strategies shared by Lavoie highly benefit students with learning disabilities—yet the knowledge of development and the ideas he shared about the necessary teacher skill-sets needed benefit all students. Lavoie claimed that perception is at the core of what motivates a student to learn. It is one thing to see images, outlined notes, or a teacher standing and speaking—but it is another thing to perceive. When we perceive, we bring meaning to whatever it is that is presented to us. So . . . are teachers providing opportunities for students to just see the content—or meaningfully perceive it? Lavoie claimed that motivation is the most misunderstood concept—is a student really disengaged because he is not motivated? Or is it because the teacher(s) did not provide the opportunities for the student to make sense of the material the teacher presented?

Quick Check—What Do You Think?

Are you and your co-teacher making time for students to perceive the ideas and information you present? Can you think of a student in your class who appears to be unmotivated? Is there something you could do to maximize his or her ability to perceive rather than detach from learning? Consider this for a moment before reading on. Jot your thoughts down to begin this thought journey. What does your co-teacher think?

Strategies to Guide Perception and Increase Motivation

Making time to provide opportunities for students to deepen their understandings could greatly increase their attention, engagement, and learning outcomes. It could most certainly cut back on the need for re-teaching and extra help sessions, since they will have time in class—within the actual instructional moments—to process, connect, and deepen their understandings. The following suggested strategies are a perfect bridge between the content you are presenting and the individual abilities and attitudes of each learner. These strategies remind teachers to make the most efficient use of the instructional time by creating the access students need to make sense of material.

Three-Minute Pause (Wiggins & McTighe, 2005)
This 3-minute strategy is perfect as a whole class, small group, or individual check-in with students. It provides the time for students to construct meaning from information presented. It encourages students to engage in the moments of learning by manipulating the material in ways that makes sense for each learner.

How the Three-Minute Pause Works

Students have the option to:

1. Summarize key facts so far.
2. Add their own thoughts as they connect with an idea presented. Ask students: What connections can you make? What does this remind you of? What can you add?
3. Pose a clarifying question. Are there words, phrases, or ideas that are not clear? What question comes to mind? Can you predict what we will talk about next?

Maslow and Motivation

As we peel back the layers of effective teaching and co-teaching, we need to return to Abraham Maslow. Remember from Chapter 2, Maslow's hierarchy of needs theory suggested that individuals are motivated to varying degrees by a combination of physiological, safety, security, and belonging needs. Each student in our classrooms has a unique set of motivators that drives his thoughts and desires into action steps. Lavoie (2007) shared eight "motivational forces" that inspire individuals to not only take action, but to also put forth the sustained effort to see a task through with the best of one's abilities (p. 98). Lavoie's eight Motivational Forces (pp. 97–106) include:

1. **Gregariousness: The Need to Belong**: This person is motivated by being surrounded by friends and feeling a sense of belonging within a crowd. The results could be popularity and friendliness, or it could take a negative turn where the individual becomes part of a negative crowd and defies authority.
2. **Autonomy: The Need for Independence**: This individual is motivated by working independently. He or she would rather work alone than participate in group work. They are inspired by the perspectives of others, but prefer to work alone.
3. **Status: The Need to Feel Important:** These individuals closely link their self-esteem with what others think about them. This person may become very focused on the viewpoints of others—he or she is eager to please others in order to convince others of their worth. These individuals are extremely sensitive to criticism—even if it is meant to be constructive.
4. **Inquisitiveness: The Need to Know**: This individual is motivated by curiosity and a genuine desire to learn and increase his or her knowledge base and understanding. This person is eager to synthesize new information with prior knowledge and experiences. He or she is very interested in the *how* and *why* of rules, procedures, or sequences of events.
5. **Aggression: The Need to Assert:** This motivator may be positive or negative depending on the individual. This person may translate his or her

energy into a positive leadership role or it may translate into the profile of a bully. Aggressive people are interested in increasing their sphere of influence and strive to have their feelings and their opinions recognized and responded to.

6. **Power: The Need for Control:** This individual is driven by his or her need to influence others. This does not have to be a negative trait. These individuals may have a strong sense of self—or a weak self-esteem. Their feelings may stem from feelings of confidence and superiority—or come from a place of feeling helpless and inferior.

7. **Recognition: The Need for Acknowledgement:** Most people are motivated by the need to be recognized for their accomplishments. (I connect this motivational force with Maslow's hierarchy as people connect belonging with being recognized). How many classroom teachers use this force as a motivator? Just think about it . . . bulletin boards with "best student of the week" or "top scores for test takers." Think of how many colleagues do you know (maybe even you)—who just love getting those "teacher of the year" or "best teacher, EVER!" cards, statues, and stickers. People all need to be acknowledged. Keep in mind this does not mean that recognition-driven people are egotists or boasters—some people just have a greater need to be recognized than others.

8. **Affiliation: The Need to Associate and Belong:** These individuals need to have strong connections with others—and with organizations— movements—and institutions. They gather great strength from the relationships they cultivate through these affiliations.

Applying the Motivating Forces: A Self-Disclosure Exercise

Lavoie encourages a self-disclosure exercise that involves you reading each description and rating yourself on a scale of 1 through 10, where 10 is highly motivated, 0 is not motivated, and 5 would indicate that you are somewhat motivated by this category.

Turn this exercise into another co-teaching relationship builder! Analyze your own profile and then share and discuss. Then discuss the meaning behind your profiles. How can each of you maximize what you learn about yourself—and each other—into meaningful, productive co-teaching steps? Jot down the results of your discussion here—how can you translate your motivational forces into your classroom—with and for students—and each other?

Valuing Learner Variability and Unique Motivational Profiles

There are many reasons why students differ in their academic performance. For example, students are variable in their cognitive abilities and home-life experiences, along with personality traits that shape their attitudes and abilities. Motivation is perhaps one key source of this variation in students' academic performance (Bandura, 2005). Students' beliefs about themselves, their environment, and the requirements for intellectual success can influence their motivation and, as a result, their performance in school (Dweck & Leggett, 1988). Let's consider the responsibility co-teachers have in shaping these beliefs—and how teachers can potentially positively affect students' academic motivation and performance.

We can connect our thinking about how students differ with Lavoie's eight motivational forces. Lavoie shared his experiences in conducting the self-disclosure exercise with hundreds of people and no one's profile matched any other profile (Lavoie, 2007, pp. 105–106). As mentioned earlier, each individual has a different set of motivators that inspires him to take action. What are the implications for teachers? Let's consider the fact that each student in your classroom has a unique set of motivational forces that motivate him or her to push through challenges and embrace new learning capabilities. It is crucial that teachers be mindful not to place students into motivational categories. Do not label students as "the gregarious boy" or "the inquisitive child." Individuals demonstrate traits of a variety of motivational forces over time and in different contexts. For example, a student may be motivated recognition when he is in physical education class striving to claim his title as the fastest runner. Yet, in social studies class, that same child may be motivated by aggression/assertiveness as he participates in a debate activity. And that very same student may easily be motivated by inquisitiveness in science class as he goes through the scientific method to prove his hypothesis. Motivational factors and individuals are too complex to be forced into any label or category. No. Never let yourself get caught in that trap. Rather—think about the concept of learner variability to drive your acceptance to embrace the natural variability that exists and unfolds within the context of your lessons each day.

Shift From Individual Differences to Predictable Variability

Meyer, Rose, and Gordon (2014) recommend embracing each student in your room through his or her patterns of strength and areas of need along the three brain networks (discussed in Chapter 1). Individual qualities are acknowledged, yet it is an overwhelming task to meet the individual needs of every student each day—especially for teachers who have a new group of students entering the classroom every time the bell rings—that's over 100 students! A focus solely on the individual qualities can easily force teachers along the deficit model view with an emphasis on what is "typical" and "atypical." Another potential concern when an individual difference view alone is embraced is the hazards of thinking that students have the same motivational and learning profiles all the time—but we now know through neuroscience research that is just not true. Individuals evolve over time—and across settings. Our learning needs and motivations vary according to the context. So a student who is a strong gregarious, visual learner in one class—on a certain day— will likely be motivated and need another learning style modality another day—or within another lesson context on the same day. How do we know this? Research provides an evolved and current view into understanding individual differences— it is through an awareness of predictable natural variability (Meyer, Rose, & Gordon, 2014). The three brain networks allow educators to think in patterns. Similar to Lavoie's motivational forces where students cannot be cornered and labeled by one motivational force for every instance for all of time, learners cannot be seen as a certain type of learner—labeled and pushed along the instructional conveyor belt. We must be flexible in understanding the depths and possibilities of an individual's abilities. So as teachers plan, they acknowledge the individual strengths and needs, but they look for patterns within the natural variability of each class-full of students. And with two teachers in the room—oh, the potential for expanding learning opportunities goes far and wide!

Planning With the Three Brain Networks in Mind—It's the UDL Way!

We know that every learner—every individual brain—has three brain networks that can guide our instructional decisions to meet the needs each student while we focus on the patterns of learning that naturally exist—we can apply our knowledge of variability—and before you know it, you no longer need to categorize learners by forcing them into one type of learning style or one type of motivational style—and certainly not by disability category. No. As Universal Design for Learning (Chapter 1) validates, viewing students through the natural variability allows learners with disabilities, gifts and talents, English Language Learners, and any other marginalized group—to come out of the sidelines and be a part—yes, a *natural part*—of the variability that exists in any population (Rose & Meyer, 2002). In addition, when teachers embrace the natural variability, they know that students are variable within themselves—their needs change and their styles change depending on the context of the learning experience. Viewing students as variable learners breaks down many academic and social barriers that result from categorizing learners into unnecessary groups based on learning deficits, styles, or motivational forces. Co-teachers experience a greater degree of variability within their classrooms. Making sure each teacher plays an active role in the process is necessary to truly meet the needs of everyone (Stein, 2016).

Getting Started With Motivating Students Through the Lens of Variability

As discussed in Chapter 1, effective instruction begins with teachers knowing their students—acknowledging their individual traits. Let's step it out for a clear image for how you and your co-teacher may apply. We begin with a linear view of the three brain networks and learner variability.

As teachers embrace variability, the UDL Principles can create a natural cycle of learning where co-teachers consider the multiple ways they can motivate and guide learners to become self-motivated learners.

Figure 4.2 Three Brain Networks and Learner Variability

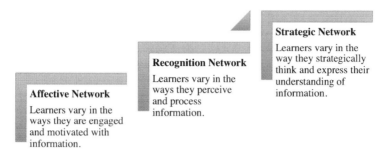

Strategic Network

Learners vary in the way they strategically think and express their understanding of information.

Recognition Network

Learners vary in the ways they perceive and process information.

Affective Network

Learners vary in the ways they are engaged and motivated with information.

Figure 4.3 The UDL Principles Become a Powerful Cycle Through the View of Variability

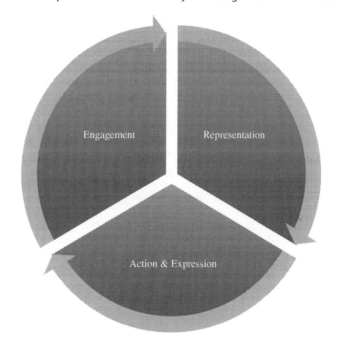

Engagement

Representation

Action & Expression

Tips to Spark Motivation With UDL in Mind

Provide Choice

Whenever possible—while staying firm with keeping to the same goal and high standards for everyone. For example, everyone must write a main idea paragraph—that is the goal. Yet, you may provide choice along the process of how to get there. Some examples of choice may include:

◆ Students may sketch or outline ideas before writing (visual).

◆ Students may discuss ideas before writing (oral).

◆ Students may watch teacher-selected short video clips to reinforce concepts before writing (multi-media).

Encourage Student Voices

Embed opportunities for each to share his or her thinking around a topic.

Introduce Realia

Bring in authentic objects for students to explore that relate to the content area topic. For example, a copy of a real diary is an interesting motivator when teaching about primary documents in social studies.

Initiate Movement

Take brain breaks through movement—get creative—incorporate jumping jacks—or integrate movement with your choice of co-teaching models as students move from station to station in small group learning activities.

Create Checklists

Either provide a checklist for students or have them create their own list to indicate the steps needed to complete a task. As they complete each step and check it off as complete—watch the motivation unfold!

Reflect

Time to pause and consider your thoughts and connections so far. What was one "a-ha" moment for you in this chapter? What is one concept you would like to transform into action steps? How do you connect this thought with something else you read in another chapter? What is one way you may apply this new idea into your teaching cycle? How will you and your co-teacher each take an active role toward this new implementation?

Mind Mapping and Motivation

This is a good time to return to an important question: *How do we actually guide students to become self-motivated?* It's one thing for teachers to understand the knowledge of theories and strategies, but it's another to actually put it into place—with real results. It seems to me that the aim is to get students to apply organized thinking that starts with a clear goal and focus—as well as the ability to monitor his or her performance along the way. A simple mind-mapping exercise can help us to achieve our aim. A mind mapping strategy is a powerful way to incorporate the ideas shared in this chapter because it takes into account the neuroscience research and motivational factors needed to entice and captivate learners.

What Is Mind Mapping?

A mind map is a multidimensional way of organizing our thinking by combining words and images through classifying ideas. Mind maps are graphic techniques that optimize the full potential of the brain's capabilities. The process of creating a mind map involves the person reflecting on information, evaluating the important details and main ideas, and then translating that into a visual or image that one can easily connect with. It is a highly personal experience of making sense of information. Mind mapping is a metacognitive activity that cultivates learning through a deep sense of awareness of one's responsibility to take charge of his learning (Buzan & Buzan, 1996).

Mind Mapping Exercise

The goal is to guide each learner to be motivated through an intrinsic drive that is sparked by you and your co-teacher designing the learning environment.

How the Mind Mapping for Motivation Exercise Works

1. **Set Goal:** This step may be completed at the beginning of the process or the end. Sometimes it is helpful to set the foundation first. And sometimes it is best to set the goal first—beginning with the end in mind.
2. **The Foundation:** Students set an intention and share an overall vision by expressing their views of themselves as learners. What is one positive learning trait?
3. **Take Action:** What small steps can be taken toward acting upon your intention and view of your positive learning trait(s)? How does this connect with your goal?
4. **Reinforce the Goal:** How does the goal fit with your intention, vision, and action steps? What motivates you to persist and achieve this goal?
5. **Create:** Students are free to sketch in color or black and white—or to write out their visual map in order to spark their ability to be self-motivated.

Some students will benefit to see the steps for this mind mapping exercise in a visual format—see Figure 4.4.

Figure 4.4 Visual for Mind Mapping Process

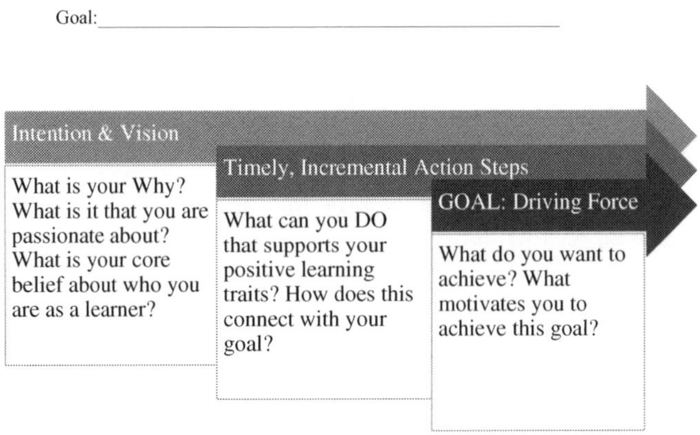

Goal:_____

Intention & Vision		
	Timely, Incremental Action Steps	
		GOAL: Driving Force
What is your Why? What is it that you are passionate about? What is your core belief about who you are as a learner?	What can you DO that supports your positive learning traits? How does this connect with your goal?	What do you want to achieve? What motivates you to achieve this goal?

Here is example from a sixth grade student who applied a mind map to motivate himself to read a one-page social studies article during an in-class assignment.

This mind map was the result of my sharing the visual steps to mind mapping (see Figure 4.4). I talked him through the guided questions. Of course when it came to the first part of setting the intention and vision of himself as a learner, this student focused on the negative view of being a "bad reader." I simply responded to that by inquiring—"OK, but what do you do well? What is it about yourself that you know you can always count on?" His response was beautifully candid and filled with a sense of hope . . . and the vision this mind-mapping exercise strives to achieve. He replied, "I am always willing to try until I get too tired and have to give up." I had him circle the "willing to try" as a visual reminder to focus on the positive. He then mapped out the steps he felt he could take to achieve his goal of reading the text. After each paragraph, a low audible "Yes!" could be heard as he clearly felt the incremental steps of success. He and I also shared plenty of affirming smiles from across the room. When the task was completed, he said to me that he looked at his mind map anytime he felt like giving up—and it made him push through. The strategy of chunking the text by reading one paragraph at a time helped him along with the skill of underlining key ideas that he felt were important. He was so proud of himself for reading the whole text on his own. He said, "Usually I just procrastinate—I know that because that's what my mom tells me I do anytime I have to read. She will really like that I didn't procrastinate today!"

Figure 4.5 Student Sample Mind Map

☑ Co-Teaching Connections

Select three to five ideas from this chapter and share how you may connect each with your co-teaching experience. How does it connect with what you are already doing? How could you extend and apply in your classroom? What could it look like? What would the students be doing? Describe the role of your co-teacher—and describe your role in the process. Share ideas with your co-teacher—and listen to his or her ideas as well—and let the co-teaching connections begin!

☼ Key Ideas

To reach all learners in the classroom, co-teachers should consider embracing the multi-dimensional view of teacher knowledge through a Pedagogical Content Knowledge lens. While grasping a clear hold of the content and subjects they teach, educators must also embrace the knowledge of students, curriculum, contexts, and methodologies as they co-create a meaningful learning environment through a co-teaching partnership—with students.

Broaden your view of the role perception plays in motivating students to take charge of their learning. Consider how you may design instruction to support learners' understanding and connection to the content. The Universal Design for Learning (UDL) Guidelines—specifically, the principle of Engagement and its Checkpoints—can serve as a valuable tool when designing and implementing information in ways to inspire self-motivation.

Consider the purposes of motivation and how they fit with learners' profiles as you work to transfer the responsibility of motivating and learning to the students as a shared process in order to inspire them to become active learners.

Remember that learning happens within the context of a lesson on any given day and time. Individuals are not defined by one category of motivational forces or by one type of learning style. Students' needs depend on the context of the learning environment—on any given day or time.

Students should be embraced as individuals within the natural variability that exists in any population. Teachers can optimize lesson design and implementation through this view of predictable variability.

Create a map to motivate and success—naturally embed timely steps to create a sense of achievement along the path of accomplishing goals.

References

Bandura, A. (2005). The evolution of social cognitive theory. In K. G. Smith & M. A. Hitt (Eds.), *Great minds in management* (pp. 9–35). Oxford: Oxford University Press.

Buzan, T., & Buzan, B. (1996). *The mind map book: How to use radiant thinking to maximize your brain's untapped potential.* New York, NY: Plume.

CAST (2011). *UDL guidelines 2.0.* Wakefield, MA: Author.

Dweck, C. S., & Leggett, E. L. (1988). A social-cognitive approach to motivation and personality. *Psychological Review, 95*(2), 256.

Fisher, D., & Frey, N. (2007). *Checking for understanding: Formative assessment techniques for your classroom.* Alexandria, VA: Association for Supervision and Curriculum Development.

Glynn, S. M., Duit, R., & Thiele, R. B. (1995). Teaching science with analogies: A strategy for constructing knowledge. In S. M. Glynn & R. Duit (Eds.), *Learning science in the schools: Research reforming practice* (pp. 247–273). Mahwah, NJ: Lawrence Erlbaum.

Himmele, P., & Himmele, W. (2011). *Total participation techniques: Making every student an active learner.* Alexandria, VA: Association for Supervision and Curriculum Development.

Johnson, D. W., & Johnson, F. (2009). *Joining together: Group theory and group skills.* (10th ed.). Boston: Allyn & Bacon.

Lambert, D. (2009). Why subjects really matter: A personal view. Retrieved from www.geography.org.uk/gtip/thinkpieces/educationalpotential/

Lavoie, R. D. (2004). *How difficult can this be?: Understanding learning disabilities: Frustration, anxiety, tension, the F.A.T. city workshop.* Alexandria, VA: Artwork PBS Video, Eagle Hill School Outreach., & Peter Rosen Productions.

Lavoie, R. D. (2007). *The motivation breakthrough: 6 secrets to turning on the tuned-out child.* New York, NY: Touchstone a Division of Simon and Schuster.

Lin-Siegler, X., Dweck, C. S., & Cohen, G. L. (2016). Instructional interventions that motivate classroom learning. *Journal of Educational Psychology, 108*(3), 295.

Meyer, A., Rose, D., & Gordon, D. (2014). *Universal design for learning: Theory and practice.* Wakefield, MA: CAST.

Ofsted (2011). Geography learning to make a world of difference. Retrieved from www. ofsted.gov.uk/resources/geography-learning-make-world-of-difference

Palmer, D. (1996). Assessing students using the 'POE'. *Investigating, 12*(3), 22.

Shulman, L. S. (1986). Those who understand: Knowledge growth in teaching. *Educational Researcher, 15*(2), 4–14.

Shulman, L. S. (1987). Knowledge and teaching: Foundations of the new reform. *Harvard Educational Review, 57*(1), 1–23.

Stein, E. (2016). *Elevating co-teaching through UDL.* Wakefield, MA: CAST.

Rose, D. H., & Meyer, A. (2002). *Teaching every student in the digital age: Universal design for learning.* Alexandria, VA: Association for Supervision and Curriculum Development.

Wiggins, G. P., & McTighe, J. (2005). *Understanding by design.* Alexandria, VA: Association for Supervision and Curriculum Development.

Wormeli, R. (2009). *Metaphors & analogies: Power tools for teaching any subject.* Portland, ME: Stenhouse.

5

Engaging Learners Through Captivating Co-Teaching: Strategies for Engagement

Essential Questions

1. What part do emotions play in the learning process?
2. How can co-teachers embed social emotional learning strategies and structures to strengthen learning experiences?
3. How can co-teachers cultivate self-regulated learners?

Emotions as a Natural Part of the Learning Process

In general, society as a whole has separated emotions from cognition. Traditionally, emotions have been treated as a construct that should be kept silent and contained in order to make way for more rational, cognitive thinking skills (Meyer, Rose, & Gordon, 2014). In the recent years, research in emotional awareness within learning environments has provided a deeper understanding into the role that emotions play in positively impacting the learning process. Loia and Senatore (2014) found that identifying emotional states within textual information guides readers to adapt their thinking to create a positive influence on their decision making processes. Pekrun et al. (2011) demonstrated that emotions, such as anxiety, pride, anger, hope, relief, and boredom, greatly impact students' thinking and information processing. Let's pause a moment. Think about your classroom experiences. Those students who demonstrate clear boredom and indifference, or excitement and anticipation, set the stage for the amount of information they will perceive and make meaningful. The students who are bored have made the decision to stay detached. Sure, teachers can influence and hopefully redirect—yet there's more teachers can do. Kordaki, Siempos, and Daradoumis (2011) claimed students' performance increased when teachers provided affective feedback and highlighted emotional awareness within a student-centered, constructivist approach to learning. Teacher comments included "What do you think about . . ." "What do you think the next step should be?" Affective feedback could be a powerful "I notice your mind seems to be somewhere else . . . what can we do to help you refocus on this class assignment?"

Providing specific, mastery-oriented feedback is also an important part of the process in blending emotions with cognitive tasks. Rosenshine (1997) supported the presence of increased student learning when teachers implemented a blending of cognitive and collaborative learning strategies within a student-centered learning environment. In an interview with *Education Week* (2014), David Rose, co-founder of the Center for Applied Specialized Technology (CAST), shared how Universal Design for Learning guides educators to cultivate the necessary emotional side of learning. In thinking about classrooms for the present and the future, Rose (2014, July 18) stated,

> I hope classrooms will have more emotion in them. That is, you'd see kids excited about learning, you'd see kids arguing various points, you'd see them questioning propositions. You'd see the stuff that really makes learning happen as opposed to the passivity we often see now. So many schools today are rule-bound, flat, vapid places. And everything we know about neuroscience tells us that that's not a good way to learn.

Co-teachers can easily consider ways to ramp up the learning in their classroom—to meet the natural variability and greater diverse populations of students by creating the space for emotions as a natural part of their instructional cycle. Teachers who say, "There's no time for that," simply need to take a step back. Reflect on the evidence that emotions are present in the learning process naturally. It comes down to the basic question: *Would you rather an emotional environment where students are passive, bored, detached— or where they are learners who express excitement, engagement, and wonder, demonstrating an active role in their learning process?* The question is not whether or not there is time for emotions in learning. The question is simply: *What range of emotions will you make the time for as you design and execute meaningful learning experiences with your students?* One way to organically blend emotions into the instructional mix is by providing affective feedback.

Tips for Blending Emotions With Cognition Through Affective Feedback

- ◆ **Be Specific:** Co-teachers can work together to be objective listeners for one another. If you hear one of you saying, "Great job!" or "No, your response does not answer the question," send out the flashing alerts! Gently support one another to fine-tune and extract the most value from giving feedback. Make time to connect with each other outside of class to guide one another to provide more specific feedback: "Great job—you found meaningful text evidence to support the theme." Or: "You're on the right track! What part of your answer begins to respond to the question? What other details do you think you could add?" As you and your co-teacher develop a strong relationship, you may even provide specific feedback to one another in the moment! Why wait to discuss outside of class? Jot down a note and discreetly pass it along. You can also create a feedback code that only you and your co-teacher will understand. It could be a symbol or word that reminds each of you, in the moment, to provide specific feedback with your students. Beginning feedback with "I notice . . ." is a powerful way to let your students know that their efforts and thoughts are valued—it can be very motivating and spark them to keep going!

◆ **Be Timely:** Make the most of the moments—timely feedback plays a key role in a student's ability to meaningfully learn and transfer knowledge and skills within the processes of learning from mistakes and celebrating successes.

◆ **Highlight Progress Toward Goal:** Remember the value of feeling successful along the way; it provides motivation for persisting through the process. In addition, learners need to remember why they need to actively participate—they need to know why their efforts matter. Talk about creating resilient learners!

◆ **Encourage Autonomy:** Respect and cultivate abilities and capabilities. No hovering! Balance your genuine desire to nurture a self-directed learner. Feedback that is too frequent may adversely affect the students' self-esteem, confidence, and independence.

◆ **Include Students in the Feedback Process:** When students are a part of evaluating their performance, they develop a keen self-awareness of their learning behaviors that are successful, so they may repeat them. They also are able to view their mistakes as a natural part of the process—and they respond effectively with strategies that help them to grapple with obstacles along the way. Co-teachers can expand the feedback process by inviting students to provide peer feedback in ways that focus on growth in a non-evaluative, non-judgmental manner. It's a win-win-win!

◆ **Give an Example:** Have peers work together to provide peer support and modeling. Students of all abilities are capable of being in a peer modeling position. If a student requires one-on-one support with a teacher following the teacher modeling, have that student, in turn, be a peer tutor to model for another peer. It is an inspiring way to create a strengths-based view of the learners in your room.

◆ **Be Sensitive to the Unique Needs of Learners—Keep Variability in Mind:** The variability of learners presents with great diversity in inclusive settings. Co-teachers must remain mindful to provide additional supports as needed. Dinham (2007) identified four questions that will help teachers to provide quality student feedback: 1. *What can the student do?* 2. *What can't the student do?* 3. *How does the student's work compare to grade level expectations and peers?* 4. *What does the student need to do better?* This is a great time to add in providing feedback through a Universal Design for Learning (UDL) lens. Another question that teachers must consider is: *How can we design instruction so that the environment and curriculum is accessible to the student?* For example, let's consider Gregory in math class.

Gregory is able to read through the word problem and identify the mathematical operations needed to solve the problem. He has difficulty remembering his basic computational facts. He needs to combine his ability in mathematical logical thinking with gaining a stronger foundation for basic math facts. If Gregory was given a calculator, he would be fine. But that access is not always permissible. Gregory must strengthen his basic facts for computations. Through a UDL lens, the environment can be designed to support Gregory. If a calculator is not permitted, he may be given additional time and access to a visual multiplication chart to guide his thinking. For a true UDL experience, all supports are available to any learner who needs additional visual supports. Gregory's need to strengthen his computational skills is not highlighted as a deficit—his skills are considered part of the natural variability that exists in any population.

◆ **Keep a Progress Notebook:** Co-teachers gear up to guide students to self-monitor their learning. And what better way to accomplish that then to co-create a system of tracking their progress together! Invite an individual student to keep a notebook to document his or her progress along the way. Keep track of goals, specific feedback, and work samples. You could even keep it digital. Open up Google Docs with your student. It would be a powerful way for you and your student to stay connected in and out of class as well.

As you read through these tips, are you feeling the opportunities to co-create relationships with your co-teacher, with your students—and with the learning process itself? Pause to share how you could add on to your current feedback practices.

_____

_____

_____

_____

Embedding Emotions Within Instruction

Well-planned co-teaching can lead to significant gains in academic, social, and communicative achievements for students—and for the two teachers in the room. Helms, Alvis, and Willis (2005) described co-teaching as an interactive, participatory experience. As teachers employ the various co-teaching models (see Chapter 1), both teachers and students co-create a great deal of interaction, dialogue, and shared learning experiences. Davis (1995) showed that students benefit from these collaborative and comprehensive teaching methods. Let's pause a moment to consider your stance on the role emotions play in the process of learning. Think about those students who appear bored and indifferent and those on the other side of the spectrum—students who are excited and engaged. What do you do to take their emotions into consideration within your instructional decisions?

_____

_____

_____

_____

How does your own emotional stance impact student learning? At this point, what do you think you and your co-teacher can do—as a team—to further embed and positively impact the social and emotional learning in your classroom?

_____

_____

What Is Social Emotional Learning?

According to Collaborative for Academic, Social, and Emotional Learning (CASEL, 2017), social and emotional learning (SEL) is the process through which individuals gain and "effectively apply the knowledge, attitudes, and skills necessary to understand and manage emotions, set and achieve positive goals, feel and show empathy for others, establish and maintain positive relationships, and make responsible decisions." CASEL has identified five unified and interconnected sets of cognitive, affective, and behavioral competencies that can easily serve to guide co-teachers to co-create a learning environment where learners have all their needs met (remember Maslow?!) as they deepen their content knowledge base.

CASEL Five SEL Components

Self-Awareness: The ability to accurately recognize one's emotions and thoughts and their influence on behavior. This includes accurately assessing one's strengths and limitations and possessing a well-grounded sense of confidence and optimism.

Self-Management: The ability to regulate one's emotions, thoughts, and behaviors effectively in different situations. This includes managing stress, controlling impulses, motivating oneself, and setting and working toward achieving personal and academic goals.

Social Awareness: The ability to take the perspective of and empathize with others from diverse backgrounds and cultures, to understand social and ethical norms for behavior, and to recognize family, school, and community resources and supports.

Relationship Skills: The ability to establish and maintain healthy and rewarding relationships with diverse individuals and groups. This includes communicating clearly, listening actively, cooperating, resisting inappropriate social pressure, negotiating conflict constructively, and seeking and offering help when needed.

Responsible Decision Making: The ability to make constructive and respectful choices about personal behavior and social interactions based on consideration of ethical standards, safety concerns, social norms, the realistic evaluation of consequences of various actions, and the well-being of self and others (CASEL, 2017).

As students are exposed to the social emotional competencies, they increase their ability to participate in learning experiences and their general capacity to learn (Durlak et al., 2011). Durlak et al. (2011) found that students increased academic achievement and social emotional skills, improved their view of themselves as learners, improved positive peer interactions, and decreased stress and misbehaviors when they participated in learning with the SEL competencies embedded within the process.

SEL is the perfect way to consider blending the emotional-affective side of learning with the cognitive-academic side of educating the whole person. When students develop social emotional competencies, they are more capable of seeking help when needed, managing their own emotions, recognizing the emotions of others, and problem solving challenging situations (Romasz, Kantor, & Elias, 2004). As co-teachers support learning within the variability in their classrooms, SEL could serve to expand possibilities and promote inclusive, positive relationships. Embedding SEL competencies each day could powerfully develop children's ability to recognize and manage emotions, build relationships, solve interpersonal problems, and make effective decisions. The following tips for embedding SEL competencies will be a part of the learning experience—it will never be a separate aspect of the learning process. Rather, emotions and cognition naturally blend and flow within any lesson—any subject—any day.

Joshua Hendrickson (personal communication, 2014, July 14), LMSW, a social-and-emotional learning consultant and the executive director of Project Presence, shares his view of co-teaching as a being *with* one another. It is common to hear teachers say that they "push-in" to classrooms to describe how co-teachers work together. The language itself can set the stage for one teacher feeling like an outsider. Unfavorable emotions may result as one teacher feels like he or she is intruding. Co-teaching is about being with: with one another and with the learning process. Inclusive, welcoming, and positive emotions have the space to emerge as co-teachers embrace a connected sense that will empower students' sense of being a part of a learning community that is all about relationships.

SEL in the Classroom: Strategies to Increase Students' Capacity for Learning and Tips for Building Relationships

◆ **Meet and Greet:** Both co-teachers could be ready at the door (or at least one teacher if one is needed to do some last-minute prep—that's one of the perks of having two teachers!) as students walk in—you will be surprised how this energized hello and simple smile will go a long way to making each student feel welcomed and an important part of the group.
   SEL Competencies Supported: Relationship Building, Social Awareness

◆ **Set High Expectations for All Learners:** Maintaining the same high expectations for all learners is a critical awareness for co-teachers to remember—and to consistently apply. Remember to keep the academic learning objectives the same—while you may scaffold and support learning through a flexible process to meet the needs of variable learners. For example, if the goal is that all students will solve the mathematical equation or word problem, then plan your instructional strategies to provide options for students to have the choice to work in pairs or on their own. Provide options for students to review the process by viewing a quick video clip online that reteaches the process. Provide options for students to work with one of the teachers to reteach. The idea is make the process flexible—while staying true to maintaining achieving the academic goal of solving the math equation.
   SEL Competencies Supported: Self-Awareness, Self-Management, Responsible Decision Making

◆ **Listen, Listen, Listen To Each and ALL:** How often do teachers get caught up in the responsibility to teach a certain aspect of the content at the expense of connecting with students? You know what I mean—it's those times when you feel the pressure of making sure you do your share to relay the necessary facts and concepts so your students will be ready for their homework, for the next lesson, for the test . . . and for moving through the grades toward graduation day! Let's bring it back to any given day in your class. What can you do to make time to listen—really listen to each student? Think about the ways you may promote the opportunity for each learner to express his thoughts—to feel heard—and listened to (consider the difference between being heard . . . and being listened to!). And then think for a second about any student who selects to stay quiet in class. How can he or she feel *listened* to? Two simple solutions could be: 1. Make eye contact with each student. Even if a student prefers to stay silent—you will connect and make him feel a part of the learning process. Remember nonverbal cues are a powerful way to speak and be heard! 2. Use sticky notes as a powerful way to invite students to share their thoughts. Time is easily an issue, but with a sticky note, students may jot down their questions or comments and share them with you after the lesson as an additional way to provide opportunity for each learner's voice to be valued. Consider the strategies throughout this book that can serve to further answer the question of how else we can listen.

Social Emotional Competencies Supported: Self-Awareness, Self-Management, Relationship Skills, Responsible Decision Making.

◆ **Celebrate All Progress:** Remember to notice all steps toward progress with respect that each learner will achieve at different rates. You can guide students to create checklists for them to monitor their task completion. Or you and your co-teacher could provide specific mastery feedback to all students (with two teachers in the room—this is possible!). You may share this feedback by writing a note—or by speaking with each student to share the specific skill or knowledge they demonstrated well.

Social Emotional Competencies Supported: Self-Awareness, Self-Management, Relationship Building, Responsible Decision Making.

◆ **Be a Learner Yourself:** We are all learners! Remember to display that passion for learning—and for the content you are teaching. Enthusiasm is contagious! Equally as important—be humble—show the human side of who you are by modeling the fact that we—all—make—mistakes! Then model the thinking and process for pushing through challenges and learning from mistakes. Share the natural side of all meaningful learning—it is all about the process of trying, persisting, and being resilient.

Social Emotional Competencies Supported: Self-Awareness, Self-Management, Responsible Decision Making, Social Awareness, Relationship Skills.

◆ **Implement Cooperative Learning Groups:** Shake up the learning by weaving in opportunities for students to listen to the perspective of peers— along with having the opportunity to share their views within smaller groups. If you are set to keep the class in rows—you may still make time for a quick slide and share activity to have students quickly turn and talk in pair share style.

Social Emotional Competencies Supported: Self-Awareness, Self-Management, Relationship Skills, Social Awareness.

Time for SEL

It is important for teachers to realize that every class they have ever been a part of—every class they will be a part of—incorporates social emotional learning to a great extent. Imagine these two scenarios:

Class 1:
Students are sitting in rows facing the board. The teacher begins class by asking them to quiet down and clear their desks. The students view a short video clip followed by the teacher asking questions. The class unfolds into a question-answer format. The teacher asks a question—students raise their hands—teacher calls on students—class passes by with many, many students sitting quietly—unmoving—at their seats. The bell rings—the students stretch, yawn, and bolt out of class.

Class 2:
Students enter class. As the bell rings, they are greeted with a general, "How is everyone doing today?" as the teacher looks around the room making eye contact. A few students share out loud as the class quickly shifts to listening to the goal for class that day. After the teacher presents information to the students, she asks them to think about it—she invites them to speak with a peer next to them. Class continues with the teacher sharing some more information and pausing every 5–10 minutes to give students a chance to connect and process. She invites them to speak with peers—and then directs their attention back to a whole-class discussion. The teacher poses a question, but rather than calling on one student, she asks students to slide their desks together to discuss. After a few minutes, she asks groups to share out loud. Every voice is heard. Every student is listening. Each student feels valued.

Social emotional learning is present in both scenarios. It is out of our control whether or not there is time for it. Emotions are a part of human nature. Teachers do have control over *how* they will incorporate SEL. Teachers do have control over what emotional energy will be present in the room. The question becomes: *What kind of SEL teacher would you like to be in your classroom?* Emotions are present no matter how much a teacher separates the emotions from the more rational cognition. Research supports deeper engagement and desire to learn when emotions and cognition are addressed as one blended powerful process.

Strategies to Support Emotions, Relationships, and Learning: Improvisations

Improvisation, in general, requires content knowledge, collaboration, social skills, critical thinking skills, and analytical skills (McKnight & Scruggs, 2008). Doesn't that sound like the perfect teaching tool? And another great feature is that it is engaging. When improvisation is used in teaching, students have the opportunity express themselves in a variety of ways, and the teacher does not evaluate any given response but instead facilitates the improvisation process with students with the aim of guiding students toward discovery of their own knowledge (Sawyer, 2004). All students get to express themselves creatively through peer interactions while their ideas are honored, their mistakes forgiven, and learning unfolds (Koppett, 2001). Improvisational techniques are tools that can be added to any existing set of teaching strategies. They can increase students' awareness of problems and ideas at the core of content learning. Teachers who apply improvisations find a way to conceptualize and implement creative teaching within their curriculum responsibilities (Sawyer, 2004). So what does this mean for co-teachers? Let's begin with a strong, basic improvisation technique—called "Yes, And!"

"Yes, And!" Strategy (Leonard & Yorton, 2015)

> *Purpose and Process:* The essence is to focus on positive interactions while gaining new insights and information. Students interact with each other and create discussions or texts that are meaningful and engaging for them. All ideas are valued and included in the activity. No idea is evaluated—just embraced. All students feel valued and have the opportunity to take creative risks while learning new content.

The essence of "Yes, And!" is collaborative teamwork and group creativity. It is an engaging exercise that allows team members to interact with each other in a light, creative way. Students sit in a circle and build a story one sentence at a time. Each sentence must begin with "Yes, and . . . " Each sentence must refer to one statement from the previous sentence. Teachers may consider this activity to review any content area subject. For example, let's consider a review of the American Revolution. One student may say, "The American Revolution was caused by growing tensions between the patriots and the loyalists." The next student could say, "Yes, and the loyalists supported British government." The student after that could say something like, "Yes, and the British government was ruled by King George III," and so on. Because you don't know what the person ahead of you will say, you can't plan ahead. Students must think on their feet—step out of their comfort zones—to share their ideas within a friendly, respectful class discussion. If someone forgets to start their sentence with "Yes, and . . . " then the group unites as a non-judgmental and friendly buzzer by saying "Buzzzz." The person who was buzzed just tries again—remembering, this time, to begin his or her sentence with "Yes, and . . . " At any time, a participant has the choice to pass—or to repeat what the person before him said to keep the exercise moving along. If someone disagrees with the statement just spoken, that person still must begin with "Yes, and. . ." and add any corrections he or she thinks should be made. For example, in the idea above, if one student said, "Yes, and the patriots supported King George III," the next student will have to start with "Yes, and . . ." to say. . . "Yes, and . . . it's really the loyalists who supported King George III." One of the teachers or one student serves as the moderator to ensure that the conversation flows respectfully, with everyone following the procedures. When everyone has had a turn (the turn-taking can go as long as you like—but each student should have at least one turn) the moderator says, "That is the end of this story." One of the teachers or a student may serve as note-taker by either audiotaping, videotaping, or writing down the gist of the story created.

A Bonus Co-Teaching "Yes, And!" Activity

Take a few minutes to begin a co-teaching story with one co-teacher making a statement about either co-teaching in general or a specific statement that reflects your experiences together. The other co-teacher responds with "Yes, and . . ." and goes on. See what topics, feelings, and questions arise that can deepen your effective partnership in learning. Return to this activity every so often—perhaps once a month—as a valuable communication tool that is fun, engaging, and productive in co-creating a positive co-teaching relationship and teaching team with your students. Use this space to document one of your "Yes, And!" co-teaching experiences.

What have you learned about yourself and your co-teacher as a result of this activity?

Mirror (McKnight & Scruggs, 2008)

Purpose and Process: The main purpose is to encourage students to increase self-awareness and social awareness through active listening and observing skills. Students increase other skills, also, such as attention and focus, empathy, and self-confidence. This activity is also an engaging quick activity to support content learning for any grade in any subject. Students work in pairs and stand facing one another, anywhere in the room. The simple choice for them to have the freedom to go anywhere in the room will be a welcomed invitation. Getting them up and out of their seats will also do wonders for guiding student engagement. Each pair of students decide which one will be student A and which one will be student B. Tell students that student A is the person looking in the mirror, and B is the image in that mirror. Tell B to begin by creating any posture or facial expression. At the teacher's signal, A may begin to copy the movements of B. At any point, the teacher may say "freeze" to bring the attention of the class to one pair—asking the class to decide which one is the mirror. Return to the exercise as each pair switches roles, so A is the image in the mirror and B is the person who imitates the image. This mirror break can take just a few minutes to pump up the attention and engagement in the class. You may go back to your lesson—or you may weave in an added step to include your content area learning.

Additional Optional Mirror Step: You may use this mirror exercise to reinforce any content area information. You could have students act out concepts, vocabulary, events, key people in history, or a scene from a piece of literature. You could also add a little volume to the activity and make it a speaking mirror activity. Students may review vocabulary or information by having one student the information giver—and the other student the one who repeats the information for reinforcement. And don't stop there—get creative. You and your co-teacher can think of other ways to adapt this exercise to meet your needs.

Space Walk (McKnight & Scruggs, 2008)

Purpose and Process: The idea with this activity is to incorporate movement while exploring their physical space (how invigorating it will feel to get a sense of the room beyond their space by their desk!), strengthening focus, listening and following directions, self-awareness, and self-confidence. Ask students to stand up and invite them to walk around the room. While they are walking, keep talking to provide opportunities for students to focus on listening to instructions as they also focus on the exercise. Your directions could be guiding students to move to explore basic movements such as "You are trying to run in 2 feet of snow." "You are walking on a tightrope." "You are in the deep end of a swimming pool." You could also make this an exercise to explore content area material. You could invite students to move like historical figures or like characters in literature. You could also invite students to explore scenes from literature or historical events. Students could also be invited to explore landforms or simply act out emotions that you mention. The idea is that they must stay in motion through all of your directions. "Stay in motion" is a mantra that you will guide your students to remember throughout the exercise. This exercise could be a quick movement, a creative break to reactivate attention and engagement—or you may incorporate as part of your content area lesson.

String of Pearls (McKnight & Scruggs, 2008)

Purpose and Process: The purpose is to ignite creative listening and oral communication skills while also strengthening self-confidence, critical thinking skills, creative problem solving, and idea generation. Have students sit or stand in any way you prefer. They may even just stay at their seats. You may even decide to have the class separate into two groups, with each group led by one co-teacher. One student (or one teacher) begins with sharing one sentence to launch a conversation or story. Each student contributes by adding another sentence that would make sense within the context of what has been said so far—while at the same time moving the conversation or story along in a productive manner. Students may go in order—or just call out as ideas come to them. If you decide to have students call out, this adds a wonderful additional and pragmatic depth to their listening and speaking skills. Invite one student (or it may just be the student next in turn) to share the final line of the conversation or story. This student could really get dramatic by standing up to demonstrate great authority in providing a conclusion. All students will cheer at the end of this exercise—with a sense of accomplishment at this opportunity for collective voices! Of course, this is another great activity to center around a content area topic. For example, it could be a procedural conversation if speaking about how to solve a math problem, or it could be a conversation around any content area topic. Let the focus and creativity flow!

Throwing Light (McKnight & Scruggs, 2008)

Purpose and Process: The premise of this activity is to develop listening skills, focus, oral communication, critical thinking, creative problem solving, oral communication, and innovative thinking. Separate the class into two groups, several small groups, or experience the exercise as a whole class. In secret, you and your co-teacher (or two students) decide on a topic of conversation. The two people who selected the topic sit or stand in the center or at the front of the group—depending on the seating arrangements of the class. The two people begin to discuss the topic in front of everyone—but they do not mention what they are discussing. As others in the class figure out the topic, they stand (or sit) with the original two and join in on the conversation—while remembering not mention the topic directly. The original two players may ask each newcomer to jot down the topic idea or whisper it to them—to ensure accuracy. If the newcomer has not figured out the topic, he or she goes back to sitting with the rest of the class. This activity is a great review before an assessment or as an engaging way to review information for deeper understanding and transfer.

Each of the improvisation strategies can serve to liven up any lesson. The excitement of working with students in the moment adds a refreshing need for co-teachers and all learners in the room to step out of their comfort zones to play a crucial, connected active part in the learning process. Every voice is valued—every learner has the opportunity to feel a part of the natural variability as co-teachers work together to co-create a community of learners—with students. All strategies discussed so far reap additional benefits of strengthening students' motivation and thinking skills needed to take charge of their learning. Which brings us to our next topic: promoting executive function in the co-taught classroom.

What Is Executive Function?

Meet Jared. He is that student you know who needs a constant jump-start to initiate and participate in learning activities. He is consistently misplacing class materials, which results in him being unprepared most of the time. You might see him at an extra help session, but he usually forgets to come. He is well liked by peers, but is so disorganized his peers avoid being his partner during cooperative learning activities. Jared's self-confidence and view of himself as a learner are adversely affected—but he becomes aloof and redirects his frustration to become the class clown; he enjoys making people laugh and receiving high-fives from peers sitting near him. Sound like any student you know? It is completely more than possible that Jared is letting his academic abilities go to waste—simply because his executive function skills need to be fine-tuned and strengthened. And dare I say it? It's not Jared's fault. Well, not completely, anyway. What could Jared's co-teachers do to support and guide his ability to participate in learning with greater success?

Ideally, you are thinking of strategies you have read in this book so far that could easily serve to empower Jared. But let's get more specific. Let's go right to the source: Jared's executive function skills. Often times, students like Jared fall into an abyss of daily and weekly assignments. They can hardly keep up with the daily tasks, let alone the long-term assignments requiring them to strategically work toward task completion. Often times, teachers discuss the list of reasons why students like Jared fall short of succeeding to organize and follow through with tasks. Reasons such as lack of support at home, lack of effort, lack of skills, etc., become the conclusion rather than the beginning of supporting these students. Supporting executive function in the classroom could be the answer.

Meltzer (2010) defines executive function as skills that allow individuals to set goals, create a plan of action, prioritize in order to follow through with plans, organize ideas and action steps, shift thinking flexibly, grasp and manipulate information in working memory, and exercising self-monitoring skills to take charge of learning. You can think about our executive function abilities as our GPS that allows us to navigate our environment for us to make purposeful and productive decisions as we organize our way through each day. Weak executive function skills have been compared to going on a long trip—out of the country—without a map—without a plan—without an idea of a destination. Self-regulation skills are a critical executive function skill. At the most basic definition, self-regulation skills empower individuals to monitor their own behaviors and learning experiences, so they remain engaged, purposeful, and productive. Hughes and Ensor (2011) linked students' deficits in executive function with weak abilities to self-regulate. Although the specific definition and constructs of executive function have been debated, most researchers agree that it is a group of interconnected cognitive processes that include (Meltzer, 2010):

- ◆ **Planning:** making a plan to gather necessary materials and complete the many steps needed to complete a task.
- ◆ **Organizing:** organizing materials, ideas, and the physical workspace needed to work productively.
- ◆ **Prioritizing:** managing time to decide what is important to work on and figuring the amount of time needed to work on it. Deciding what information is important to remember.
- ◆ **Shifting:** thinking flexibly—being able to think about big ideas and the related details. Embracing one's perspective, while opening up to see there is another valid way of thinking about something—or another way to do something.
- ◆ **Working Memory:** perceiving information and making decisions about whether it is important to remember, interesting but not necessary to remember, or irrelevant information to be let go. Being able to perform this consistently across time, settings, content areas, situations, and tasks.
- ◆ **Checking:** reflecting along the process of learning to self-monitor one's performance and understanding. It involves thinking about the task at hand while thinking about how one is thinking and performing.

Co-Creating a Systematic Structure to Support Executive Function

It is important to remember that executive function skills are not related to intelligence. Executive function needs are not a result of a student's unwillingness to participate—these students are quite capable and are often eager to succeed. Unfortunately, sometimes they use up much of their energy trying to accomplish tasks and they are left exhausted—which can be interpreted as student indifference when it is actually just a learned behavior. What they really need is support with their executive function skills.

Let's consider Peter, a sixth grade student. He has always participated in class discussions in all content areas. His background knowledge has been deep and strong. Peers have created a nick-name for him, "the webmaster," because he is viewed as a knowledgeable resource! His teachers have been perplexed by the fact that his knowledge base has been strong—he is an active learner in class—yet he is failing his content area classes. Each teacher identifies the reason: He never completed any homework or classwork, regardless of supports provided by teachers.

By February, Peter is no longer as active in class. He has let his hair grow long so that it covers his eyes in one side-swept style. This once-active participant now slouches in his seat, apparently indifferent. Peter has not been identified as a student with special needs; his parents have been involved and are just as confused as everyone else.

It just so happens that Peter has been in an inclusive setting for two of his classes. Luckily, the teachers have worked as a team and have been able to apply a team approach to supporting him. They have brought Peter in on the process, trying to gain insights into what was going on. Finally, one day, one teacher sees Peter at his locker and pieces together the evidence. His locker contains old lunches, crushed notebooks, loose papers, and random articles of clothing from physical education class. The first step toward meaningful solutions is taken that day. The teacher suggests to Peter and his parents that he get an accordion folder to hold his loose papers that could be categorized by content area class. In addition, he is permitted to use his phone's Notes app to write down his homework each night—since his calendar/agenda is in pieces at the bottom of his locker.

You are getting the idea, right? This student had been thriving—until the world of middle school, where he was slowly swept away by the fast-paced schedule and ongoing assignments. Peter needed support with his executive function skills. Imagine if executive function skills were naturally and proactively embedded, so that students like Peter did not lose any time? Peter needed support to self-regulate.

Three Types of Executive Abilities Co-Teachers Should Support

Executive function and self-regulation skills depend on three types of brain function: working memory, mental flexibility, and self-control. These functions are highly inter-related, and the successful application of executive function skills requires them to operate in coordination with each other (Meltzer, 2010).

- ◆ **Working Memory** manages our ability to perceive, retain, and manipulate information within the moments—for short periods of time. As information is processed through working memory, an individual decides what aspects of the information will be released and what information is important to remember and transferred to long-term memory.
- ◆ **Mental Flexibility** provides the ability for individuals to sustain or shift attention in response to various demands. In addition, flexibility allows one to apply different actions based on different settings. It also allows for individuals to be open to learning new ways of thinking about ideas and new ways of acting upon ideas based on listening to the perspective of others.
- ◆ **Self-Control** creates the ability for individuals to set priorities and resist impulsive actions or responses.

TABLE 5.1 Two Categories of Executive Function Skills

Thinking Skills	Self-Regulation Skills
Planning, goal setting, organizing, prioritizing, working memory	Flexibility, self-regulation of behaviors, and task initiation and follow-through.

Another Way of Considering Executive Function Skills

Another way co-teachers may consider embedding executive function skills is to categorize the executive function skills into two main categories (see Table 5.1).

Once teachers assess the function of the student's behavior, they will be able to find a solution that meets the needs for learning to take place. Teachers can ask themselves: 1. *What skill is needed*? 2. *What do I know about this student*? 3. *What strategies could support this skill*? (Then review and consider strategies in this chapter and throughout the book to get you started!).

Teachers also must identify whether the student's behavior is a result of lack of motivation rather than lack of skill. If the student has demonstrated skill level, then teachers must wonder: 1. *Is it truly a motivation weakness—or skill weakness*? If motivation, teachers need to consider that perhaps the student is losing interest because the work is too difficult or too easy. Consider the scaffolds and strategies to support motivation from Chapter 4 as a place to begin. Consider also the amount of energy a student puts into a task. Let's consider the student who never has a pencil—or has a pencil, but needs to sharpen it every few minutes (yes! we all know those students!).

So how can co-teachers determine whether a student's behavior is a result of a lack of motivation or skill?

Robert's Spark

Robert was a seventh grade student who sat in class quietly with a consistent gaze on the teacher. Each teacher felt that Robert was paying attention. If he was called on, he was able to respond by either asking a clarifying question or by contributing his response. However, anytime writing was part of the process, Robert did not have anything to write with. He managed to break every writing utensil (a noticeable ink stain still resides on his desk from snapping the tip off a pen one day). When given a computer, he just stared at the screen—excusing himself to the men's room—or the nurse—anywhere but in the classroom. When discussing Robert, teachers would say, "He's just not motivated." "He is exhausted because he helps to take care of his little brother all night." These well-intentioned comments served as excuses for Robert's behavior. What we needed was to redirect Robert's behavior through compassionate supports. I just couldn't agree that Robert was not motivated. There was a spark in his eye in social studies class. He shared stories that his grandfather shared. Yet, when it came time to work on classwork—especially when writing was involved—spark transformed into fight-or-flight mode.

So, I sat down with Robert and complimented the strong background knowledge he shared in his classes. And I then took a leap of faith and complimented him on how motivated he was to complete class assignments. He gave me one of those looks—shocked, half laughing, and he said, "What!?!" I smiled, and said, "Yes, you are so motivated that you think of all these strategies to avoid completing the task. Your pencil or pen breaks, you need to run to your locker, the nurse, the men's room . . . anywhere but here. That takes a lot of energy and thought in achieving the goal you set for yourself—your goal of avoiding the task. It's brilliant!"

Robert said, "I don't get it. How is that a good thing?"

I said, "Think about it. All learners need to apply strategies as they learn, right?" Robert nodded. I continued, "And you are doing that brilliantly! You just need to redirect your motivation—you need to stop applying strategies for avoiding the task—and you need to apply strategies that will help you to actually DO the task." Silence. I let it sink it a minute. I said, "So how about it? Would you like to shift your strategy use from avoidance strategies to cognitive strategies that help you to get the task done?" Robert was with me then . . . the spark (luckily!) clicked. He said, "OK, how do we do that?"

We couldn't take away all of his avoidance strategies at once—if we really wanted to make him comfortable to progress in areas that caused him stress. I said, "How about if we replace one of your avoidance strategies with one strategy that will support you when we have to write in class?" I assured Robert that I, and all of his teachers, would support our plan—but the only way it would work is if he took charge of his learning. He was in agreement—we brainstormed writing strategies that he would use. He selected a strategy that allowed him to sketch and/or outline his ideas first along with applying basic graphic organizers that are offered for any student in the class. He also agreed to ask more questions either in class or during extra help sessions.

Redirecting Motivation and Self-Regulation: Strengthening Executive Function Skills

As discussed in Chapter 4, motivation is a very misunderstood construct. Students are usually motivated—the purpose and the action steps of their motivational force may need to be redirected. In Peter's case—two teachers in the room guided his progress—two varying perspectives allow for learning opportunities to unfold. As one teacher saw an unmotivated student, another teacher saw a misdirected, motivated learner who needed support to self-regulate his learning. Problem solved! It's true: The solution is not always a quick process. Co-teachers must be patient, compassionate, open to new ideas, and tenacious when sifting through the learning characteristics and abilities in each learner in the room.

What Co-Teachers Can Do: Strategies to Embed Executive Function Skills

Take a Break: Guide students' ability to self-regulate by inviting students to take a three-minute break as they need. Co-create an environment based on the trust and respect needed to just breathe. Some teachers like to use designated break cards that students place on their desk to indicate they need to pause for a few minutes. If students attempt to make the break too long, teachers should gently guide students to keep breaks to a few minutes by asking them "How much longer?" This question keeps the responsibility on the student to continue monitoring his performance. Co-teachers may also encourage whole class stretch breaks to keep everyone alert and ready to learn more.

Goal-Plan-Do Checklist: Keep students focused and on track as they monitor learning—while breaking tasks down into manageable tasks. Co-teachers may write a general Goal-Plan-Do list to give students a general sense of what is expected. For example, in English class a Goal-Plan-Do Checklist could look like this:

Goal: To gather three pieces of text evidence to support your thinking.

Plan: Reread text and notes from yesterday to review your claim/thesis statement. Annotate and underline key points to support your thinking.

Do: Write your selected three pieces of evidence from the text in your notes section.

This general checklist provides a focal point to guide any student who needs to set a clear purpose and plan to accomplish lesson expectations. Each student is invited to write his or her own checklist by breaking down the "Plan" in a more personalized, strategic manner. Bottom line: Each learner is held to the same high expectations and goal completion.

For example, a student-personalized Goal-Plan-Do Checklist could specify additional strategies within the plan: Break each section of reading into sections. Highlight the key words for each section. Another student's "Plan" could include: Reread the text by listening to the audio reading. And yet another student's plan could include "Partner read with a peer" as a viable strategy to guide comprehension and task completion.

The idea with Goal-Plan-Do is that each student adheres to the learning objectives—but has the flexibility to plan out learning steps to meet his or her personal needs for that day.

KNOW Strategy (Steinberg, 2005): Guide students to build confidence and mathematical thinking as they read math word problems. This acronym serves as an outline to support organization, memory, self-regulation, and flexibility to think about solutions. Students take the following steps:

1. Read through the word problem with fluency to gain an understanding for the context of the word problem. Guide students to see it as a story with an ending that needs to be solved.

2. Key phrases: Students underline important information. Being mindful that just key words are not enough—students need to read the key words within the context to gain a true understanding.

3. Numbers: Circle important numbers needed to solve the problem.

4. Operations: After rereading the word problem—and considering the context of the story, what mathematical operations will need to be applied? Is there more than one step or operation needed?

5. Work it out: In a systematic, step-by-step manner apply the knowledge that was gained by reading through the word problem—and solve it.

Mind Velcro: guide students to make important information stick as they listen, read, or view content. Encourage students to self-regulate their learning by asking themselves: *What do I already know? What do I need to remember that adds on to my thinking?* Students are motivated by the analogy of having Velcro in their minds—it can create a strong mindful visual cue.

☑ Co-Teaching Connections

Select three to five ideas from this chapter and share how you may connect each with your co-teaching experience. How does it connect with what you are already doing? How could you extend and apply in your classroom? What could it look like? What would the students be doing? Describe the role of your co-teacher—and describe your role in the process. Share ideas with your co-teacher—and listen to his or her ideas as well—and let the co-teaching connections begin!

☼ Key Ideas

Traditionally, emotions and cognition have been separated within the learning process to focus on more rational, cognitive thinking during the learning process in the classroom.

Providing specific, affective feedback serves to naturally blend emotions to guide learners to take charge of their learning.

Co-teachers can empower their relationships with one another, with students, and with learning itself by acknowledging the natural presence of emotions—and applying the knowledge and strategies of social emotional learning throughout the instructional design.

Executive function skills must be supported in inclusive settings to guide all learners to take control of their learning and achievements.

References

CASEL (2017). Core SEL Competencies Retrieved from http://www.casel.org/core-competencies/

Davis, J. R. (1995). *Interdisciplinary courses and team teaching: New arrangements for learning.* Westport, CT: Greenwood Publishing Group.

Dinham, S. (2007). How schools get moving and keep improving: Leadership for teacher learning, student success and school renewal. *Australian Journal of Education, 51*(3), 263–275.

Durlak, J. A., Weissberg, R. P., Dymnicki, A. B., Taylor, R. D. & Schellinger, K. B. (2011). The impact of enhancing students' social and emotional learning: A meta-analysis of school-based universal interventions. *Child Development, 82*(1), 405–432.

Helms, M. M., Alvis, J. M., & Willis, M. (2005). Planning and implementing shared teaching: An MBA team-teaching case study. *Journal of Education for Business, 81*(1), 29–34.

Hughes, C., & Ensor, R. (2011). Individual differences in growth in executive function across the transition to school predict externalizing and internalizing behaviors and self-perceived academic success at 6 years of age. *Journal of Experimental Child Psychology, 108*(3), 663–676.

Koppet, K. (2001). *Training to imagine: Practical improvisational theatre techniques to enhance creativity, teamwork, leadership, and learning.* Sterling, VA: Stylus.

Kordaki, M., Siempos, H., & Daradoumis, T. (2011). Collaborative learning design within open source e-learning systems. *e-iInfrastructures and technologies for lifelong learning: Next generation environments* (pp. 212–233). IGI Global.

Leonard, K. & Yorton, T. (2015). *Yes, and: How improvisation reverses "no, but" thinking and improves creativity and collaboration—lessons from the second city.* New York, NY: Harper Collins.

Loia, V., & Senatore, S. (2014). A fuzzy-oriented sentic analysis to capture the human emotion in Web-based content. *Knowledge-based systems, 58*, 75–85.

McKnight, K. S., & Scruggs, M. (2008). *The second city guide to improv in the classroom: Using improvisation to teach skills and boost learning.* San Francisco, CA: Jossey-Bass.

Meltzer, L. (2010) *Promoting executive function in the classroom.* New York, NY: Guilford Press.

Meyer, A., Rose, D., & Gordon, D. (2014). *Universal design for learning: Theory and practice.* Wakefield, MA: CAST.

Pekrun, R., Goetz, T., Frenzel, A. C., Barchfeld, P., & Perry, R. P. (2011). Measuring emotions in students' learning and performance: The Achievement emotions questionnaire (AEQ). *Contemporary Educational Psychology, 36*(1), 36–48.

Romasz, T. E., Kantor, J. H., & Elias, M. J. (2004). Implementation and evaluation of urban school-wide social-emotional learning programs. *Evaluation and Program, 27*(1). 89-103.

Rose, D. (2014, July 18). "I hope classrooms have more emotion in them": David Rose interviewed in Education Week. Retrieved from www.cast.org/whats-new/news/2014/david-rose-interviewed-by-education-week.html#.WHFBVbYrLow

Rosenshine, B. (1997). Advances in research on instruction. In J. W. Lloyd, E. J. Kameanui, & D. Chard (Eds.), *Issues in educating students with disabilities* (pp. 197–221). Mahwah, NJ: Lawrence Erlbaum.

Sawyer, K. R. (2004). Creative teaching: Collaborative discussion as disciplined improvisation. *Educational Researcher, 33*(2) 12–20. doi: https://doi.org/10.3102/0013189X0330002012

Steinberg, R. J. (2005). Intelligence, competence, and expertise. In A. J. Elliot & C. S. Dweck (Eds.), *Handbook of competence and motivation* (pp. 15–31). New York: Guilford Press.

Afterword

Additional Thoughts and Action Steps

Successful co-teaching involves much more than knowing and teaching content. Creating positive co-teaching relationships is a critical component for achieving and sustaining effective co-teaching practices. Both teachers should view one another as equal partners—as well as feel comfortable to actively participate in the learning process (Bouck, 2007). Rivera, McMahon, and Keys (2014) shared three actions that can lead to meaningful and effective co-teaching experiences. I've added a fourth.

1. **Engage in frequent role-switching**: The two teachers plan and implement instruction by alternating roles and responsibilities—so each teacher experiences the instructional process by focusing on the importance of teaching the content as well as supporting specific students' needs. As co-teachers reverse roles, they allow for multiple ways of presenting material and engaging students in various methods and strategies.
2. **Align philosophies on education:** Co-teachers should develop a streamlined vision for how to accommodate the curriculum for the students in their class, so that each learner has the opportunity to meet with the same high expectations. Effective use of planning time and ongoing communication and collaboration must occur on a regular basis.
3. **Remain flexible and open-minded:** Flexibility is key in order to value the diverse perspectives and expertise of both teachers. Where it is likely that a general education teacher may become territorial in his or her classroom, flexibility will release any tensions and pave the way for both teachers to be actively involved during every phase of the instructional process.
4. **Expect content mastery by the special education teacher:** Bouck (2007), as well as Dieker and Murawski (2003), expressed the importance of special education teachers embracing the content on a level where they are able to take the lead with lessons or weave in meaningful explanations and additional examples to clarify the content to support deeper understandings for all learners.

As co-teachers share an active role in the learning process, students with disabilities are given opportunities to work toward mastery in meeting the demands of challenging curriculum as well as engage in effective and purposeful peer interactions. Students have the opportunity to increase their self-efficacy as the two teachers in the room model and embrace a true inclusive mindset.

Much more than teacher support at the classroom level is needed to cultivate true and meaningful inclusive experiences. Inclusion should be embraced at the building level. The school should be a place where varied abilities are accepted, embraced, and valued. Administrators can be the driving force for creating a building-wide culture of collaboration. Each co-teaching pair should be supported in individual ways to guide successful instruction that serves all students. Co-teachers should reach out— seek out—and invite administrators' insights and ideas for mapping out successful planning and instructional routines. Administrators may serve to support co-teachers on a variety of levels:

1. Devise a schedule for time to co-plan and to ensure that the time is used in the most productive manner.
2. Mediate any co-teaching relationship concerns. For example, when co-teachers' philosophical beliefs about teaching and accommodating diverse learners arise, an administrator can serve as the objective voice to guide solutions.
3. Create meaningful professional development experiences. For example, mapping out time for co-teachers in the building to gather as a group to discuss their experiences and questions can be a powerful, authentic time for growth. In addition, administrators should devise a plan for strengthening the areas specific to each co-teaching pair. For example, if one special education teacher needs additional supports gaining content mastery and another needs support with applying strategies, the principal could encourage a process of collegial networks within the building where each co-teacher seeks out at least one colleague who can serve as a source of support. Outside training for co-teaching has an important place—but must be followed up with meaningful, in-house, job-embedded supports on an ongoing basis.
4. Classroom visits should be a natural part of the inclusive plan. Administrators should provide co-teachers with non-evaluative, formative feedback to sustain positive practices and support continued growth.
5. Maintain conversations that share effective accommodations and scaffolds to meet the needs of diverse learners—while maintaining the same high expectations for everyone.

Administrators and teachers should work together to make sure that general education teachers and special education teachers get the supports they need. For example, general education teachers should receive support in learning about varied methods of teaching to meet the needs of diverse learners. Guiding general education teachers to step out of more conventional, teacher-centered techniques with flexibility to create more student-centered and co-taught lessons can strengthen a co-teaching experience. In addition, special education teachers may need guidance in expanding their content-area mastery to ensure more effective co-teaching partnerships. Regardless of the support needed, higher degrees of collaboration serve to increase positive emotional and social supports needed to establish positive learning outcomes. When a culture of inclusion is naturally embedded within the culture of the classroom and the school as a whole, co-teachers increase their ability to diversify instructional approaches, students with disabilities gain a stronger sense of belonging, and all students have access to meaningful, challenging curriculum and learning experiences (Rivera, McMahon, & Keys, 2014).

A Structure for Success: Thinking About Next Steps

Co-teaching is a very delicately balanced phenomenon. It has the potential for great success regardless of teacher pairings as long as communication and an open-minded focus on students' success remains at the center of each teacher's mission. One of the two co-teachers, at least, must remain on a path with the attitude: *We will make it work—no matter what!* A co-teaching mindset comes easy to some and requires great change in thinking for others. At a TASH conference, Knoster (1991) shared the components for meaningful, systemic steps when implementing any needed change. Knoster described five components that can positively impact outcomes toward achieving a group's intentions and hopes for success. Knoster suggested that when vision, skills, incentives, resources, and an action plan are collectively embedded within the structure of a system, then positive change will be a likely result. However, if any of the components are missing, then the process of collaborative efforts will adversely affect the hope for meaningful change (See Table 6.1).

The application of this template, of course, becomes an adventure when working with varied personalities and the elements that make interacting with human nature so exciting. Working with groups of people just never falls into the neat boxes and flow presented in this chart. Yet, this matrix can serve as an anchor to guide administrators and co-teachers in developing a plan for purposeful and sustainable positive co-teaching experiences. The components displayed in the matrix express what is needed for success to be met. Equally as important, the matrix highlights the emotional outcomes that may arise if any one of the components is missing. During times of potential frustration, anxiety, or confusion, group leaders (that's all of you,

TABLE 6.1 The Knoster Matrix for Meaningful Change (Knoster, Villa, & Thousand, 2000)

Vision	Skills	Incentives	Resources	Action Plan	= Sustainable Change
X	Skills	Incentives	Resources	Action Plan	= Confusion
Vision	X	Incentives	Resources	Action Plan	= Anxiety
Vision	Skills	X	Resources	Action Plan	= Resistance
Vision	Skills	Incentives	X	Action Plan	= Frustration
Vision	Skills	Incentives	Resources	X	= Treadmill and False Starts

TABLE 6.2 Components of Success

Vision	Skills	Incentives	Resources	Action Plan	= SUCCESS!

co-teachers, too!) may look at the matrix for guidance for how to redirect and maintain positive action steps toward achieving the shared vision.

Maintaining a focus on the first row, I have learned, can keep the process for change visible and manageable. (See Table 6.2.) The components needed for success remain at the forefront to empower long-lasting change—even if the process may be slow—so the process has a strong chance of moving in the right direction in a meaningful, slow, but steady, pace.

Vision: Administrators and teachers join in sharing their individual views about why co-teaching is important and why each person is part of the co-teaching process. Each person should create a statement to share why and what they hope to achieve. Shared conversations in person and shared online conversations (using Google Docs, for example) must be open and ongoing. The group should co-create a shared vision that consists of one statement or brief paragraph that incorporates each viewpoint that becomes a part of the group's mission statement. The result will become the anchor—the go-to visual reminder—that will refocus the group to deal with any problems that arise along the way and will combat any confusion that may arise. This shared vision is the foundation for developing a sustainable co-teaching mindset with meaningful actionable and sustainable steps.

Skills: Teachers assess the skill sets that each brings to the co-teaching scene. As a group, administrators and co-teachers decide on the skills needed to achieve co-teaching success at the classroom level and at the building level. As the group identifies the skills that each person brings to the experience, and what additional skills are needed, a sense of empowerment begins to replace any anxiety. It's about making teaching visible and manageable—and when the specific skills are identified, each co-teacher can gain a clear focus for her/his personal role in the co-teaching equation. The skill sets mentioned in earlier chapters serve to provide a reassurance for what each teacher will need to do along the process. A calm reassurance is created as teachers embrace their skills in curriculum design, building relationships, supporting motivation and a comfortable learning environment, and establishing meaningful routines and classroom management.

Incentives: Providing the group with a reason for working toward the shared vision can resolve any push-back or resistance from colleagues and administrators. Intrinsic motivation should be the driving force. After all, the intentions should always be focused on that intangible reward of feeling the positive flow of co-creating successful co-teaching learning experiences. Yet, additional incentives are often needed. There is a need to devise some external motivation for anyone who may need an additional perk to participate in a co-teaching experience. For example, creating a schedule where the co-teachers have release time to co-plan or creating professional development where teachers receive in-service credits or a stipend can go a long way in making sure that everyone is on board with the plan.

Resources: Identifying the resources needed is a must to support each member of the group. It is important to identify tools such as iPads, Chromebooks, or other technologies available to amplify the learning process for students. A shared resource of books, articles, websites, etc., can be gathered in a place where the group may access them at anytime—for instance, in a shared Google Document and also in an accessible place in the building that stores specific book titles that support co-planning and creating positive co-teaching relationships. Keep the list ongoing where anyone in the group may access and add to it as time goes on.

Action Plan: The components for support, collaboration, and change provide the focus to motivate the group to create the steps needed to stay focused on achieving the shared vision. Delineating roles and responsibilities for each member of the group can serve to eliminate any false starts that lead to an exhausting treadmill effect. A meaningful action plan will serve to bring each member of the group together to work collaboratively and compassionately toward achieving an effective, long-lasting culture of collaboration at the classroom level—and building level. One way to devise a plan is, again, to focus on the top row of the Knoster matrix (see Table 6.3).

Once this vision is clear, the group may decide the delicate balance of making the action plan visible to educators and experienced by students.

The following Shared Vision Organizer (Table 6.4) may be used to guide the decisions toward developing positive co-teaching experiences at the classroom and

TABLE 6.3 Components of Success

Vision	Skills	Incentives	Resources	Action Plan	= SUCCESS!

TABLE 6.4 Shared Vision Organizer

	Why	What	Where	When	Who & How
Vision					
Skills					
Incentives					
Resources					
Action Plan & Next Steps					

building levels. Once the basic structure for the plan is created, more personalized and outlined steps may be created. This organizer, along with the Knoster matrix, is meant to serve as a starting point toward personalized, powerful results.

Moving the Vision

What are your personal views about successful co-teaching experiences? What does that experience look like? What needs to be in place in order for your vision to become a part of your co-teaching daily practice? In addition to your co-teacher, who are the people who could support and empower your co-teaching professional growth? How can you use the topics discussed in each chapter to fine-tune your co-teaching vision? Jot some of your ideas here—and get ready to think about how you can share your vision. Using Knoster's matrix, what could your next step be? What can you do to begin moving the vision for co-teaching success?

_____

_____

_____

_____

_____

_____

_____

_____

References

Bouck, E. C. (2007). Co-teaching... not just a textbook term: Implications for practice. *Preventing School Failure: Alternative Education for Children and Youth, 51*(2), 46–51.

Dieker, L. A., & Murawski, W. W. (2003). Co-teaching at the secondary level: Unique issues, current trends, and suggestions for success. *The High School Journal, 86*(4), 1–13.

Knoster, T. (1991). Presentation at TASH conference. *Washington, DC, 34.*

Knoster, T., Villa, R., & Thousand, J. (2000). A framework for thinking about systems change. *Restructuring for caring and effective education: Piecing the puzzle together,* (pp. 93–128). Baltimore, MD: Brookes.

Rivera, E. A., McMahon, S. D., & Keys, C. B. (2014). Collaborative teaching: School implementation and connections with outcomes among students with disabilities. *Journal of prevention & intervention in the community, 42*(1), 72–85.

Appendix 1: Glossary of Strategies Mentioned in Chapter 1

Think Aloud

Think Alouds help students learn to monitor their thinking as they engage in a lesson. Students simply allow their thoughts to be shared through conversation or in writing. This metacognitive experience allows one's ideas become visible as they share out loud or in writing. This process reveals how deeply students understand the material. Students may work in pairs to allow each student to engage in the process of deepening their understanding. Co-teachers may optimize students' ability to apply the think aloud strategy by modeling for the class.

For more information: www.teachhub.com/teaching-strategies-think-alouds

Guided Notes

Guided notes support students' abilities to determine importance when listening and/or viewing content area material. Co-teachers may alternate in modeling notes as one teacher leads a class discussion or reading of subject area materials.

For further information: www.interventioncentral.org/academic-interventions/study-organization/guided-notes-increasing-student-engagement-during-lecture-

Socratic Seminar

A Socratic Seminar approach cultivates critical thinking, speaking, and listening skills as students engage in collaborative dialogues. The goal is to encourage meaningful conversations through generating and responding to questions. Teachers pose thoughtful, open-ended questions that spark students' thinking and communication skills. Students deepen their own understanding as they learn from the perspective of others. Co-teachers may serve to model and co-facilitate deeper learning for all.

For further information: www.readwritethink.org/professional-development/strategy-guides/socratic-seminars-30600.html

Accountable Talk

Accountable talk is a collaborative discussion process that empowers each student to engage in a specific role during conversations. Students speak, listen, and extend their thinking by adding on to the thoughts of others.

Co-teachers can model and guide students' conversations through the following prompts:

I agree with you when you said. . . .
I would like to add to your thinking by. . . .
Could you clarify what you said about. . .
I disagree with you when you said. . . .because. . . .
How do you know. . . .? What evidence do you have to support your thinking about. . .?

For further information: www.theteachertoolkit.com/index.php/tool/accountable-discussions

Cooperative Learning

Cooperative learning creates a sense of community as students work together in small groups to problem solve and create results. Teachers serve as facilitators to guide learners to strengthen their intrapersonal and interpersonal skills through a variety of academic tasks.

For further information: www.co-operation.org/what-is-cooperative-learning/

Front-End Scaffolds

Front-end scaffolding is defined as the actions teachers take to prepare students to better understand how to access complex text before they read it. Traditionally, front-end scaffolding has included information to build greater context for the text, front-loading vocabulary, summarizing the text, and/or making predictions about what is to be read. Close analytical reading requires that teachers greatly reduce the amount of front-end scaffolding to offer students the opportunity to read independently and create meaning and questions first. It also offers students the opportunity to own their own learning and build stamina.

For further information: www.engageny.org/sites/default/files/resource/attachments/scaffolding_student_needs.pdf

Back-End Scaffolds

Back-end scaffolding, on the other hand, is defined as what teachers plan to do after students read complex text to help deepen understanding of the text. When teachers provide back-end scaffolds, they follow the "Release-Catch-Release model," allowing students to grapple with hard text FIRST, and then helping students as needed.

For further information, see: www.engageny.org/sites/default/files/resource/attachments/scaffolding_student_needs.pdf

Collaborative Strategic Reading

Collaborative strategic reading is a comprehension strategy that guides students to monitor their comprehension, vocabulary, and concept development through a cooperative learning activity. The four phases of the reading experience include having the students preview the text, stop to monitor their understanding through identifying "clicks and clunks," review main ideas through sharing the "gist," and summarize through the "wrap up."

For more information: www.ncset.org/publications/viewdesc.asp?id=424

Sheltered Instruction

A research-based model that encompasses eight phases toward building vocabulary and comprehension for English Language Learners and students struggling with reading, writing, listening, or speaking. The emphasis is on building students' background knowledge base as teachers strategically develop language-based lesson plans that provide meaningful supports and scaffolds toward students' personal achievement in language-based academic experiences.

For more information: www.pearsonschool.com/index.cfm?locator=PS3zZc

The Strategic Instruction Model (SIM)

The Strategic Instruction Model (SIM) is a scaffolding strategy that supports literacy development. The approach includes content enhancement routines that guide the teacher to design instruction with a learner-centered focus. Teachers present information in ways that facilitates students to connect, organize, and construct meaning. Graphic organizers and use of multi-media are examples of content enhancements. Also see the UDL Guidelines (page 16) for additional ideas for varying the ways information is presented, processed, and expressed by and with students. The SIM model embodies a learner-centered process that cultivates a sense of community, autonomy, and achievements.

For more information about the Strategic Instruction Model (SIM) visit: http://kucrl.ku.edu/sim

Appendix 2: Strategies for Building Relationships

Student Profile Sheet

Student Names	Strengths	Interests	Area of Need

Co-Teacher Profile Sheet

Each co-teacher should complete one Profile Sheet and share with one another to align along the process of co-creating a shared vision and meaningful learning environment for all learners in the room.

Name of Co-Teacher_____

	Strengths	Interests	Beliefs
Character Traits that describe and fortify my teacher self!			
Teaching Style			
Lesson Planning and Organization			
Classroom Management			

Conversation Starters!

Share one or all of the following.

1. Co-teaching is like _____ because _____.

2. Educating diverse learners in an inclusive classroom is _____

   because _____.

3. Rate the following in terms of importance and then share your reasons with your co-teacher: Communication, Organization, Connectedness

Appendix 3: Book Discussion Questions

Chapter 1

1. What strengths do you bring to your role as a teacher? How can you share one of these strengths with your students and co-teacher?
2. What strengths does your co-teacher bring to your teaching team?
3. What is one co-teaching model you are most comfortable with—and when is the last time you implemented it? Share how the lesson unfolded.
4. Think about an upcoming lesson: What is one co-teaching model that you plan to apply? How will you and your co-teacher plan to combine one another's area of expertise for that lesson?
5. Summarize your understanding of how you may gain a UDL perspective when designing your instruction.
6. Consider the students in your classroom who will need additional scaffolds through specially designed instruction. How will UDL set the stage for creating optimal access and meaning?

Chapter 2

1. Select two students in your class and discuss how Maslow's hierarchy of needs applies to these students' narratives. What do you and your co-teacher do to support these students, according to Maslow's theory? What could you do to support connected learning experiences in your classroom?
2. Review one of your reflections from this chapter—how does it connect with specific students in your class? How does it connect with your co-teaching relationship? How can you apply your reflection to empowering your relationship with your students and with each other?
3. Choose two or three strategies from this chapter that you found interesting. How could you and your co-teacher apply within the next few weeks? Discuss your specific roles for each of you.
4. Based on your reading so far, what idea, topic, or question resonates with you at this point? How can you apply this to your current experiences?

Chapter 3

1. What is one new concept you learned and found interesting? How could you apply it with your co-teacher and students?

2. How could you incorporate the co-teaching models as you consider developing your classroom management structure? Consider at least two models as you explain. And remember to vary your application of the models over the course of each month.
3. Share one strategy you read that you have already applied in class. How could you apply this strategy in a new way? What would your co-teaching roles be?
4. How does Maslow's hierarchy once again bring importance to creating meaningful learning environments? What specific idea or strategy discussed in this chapter connects with support for the necessity for teachers to bring Maslow's ideas into authentic action steps?

Chapter 4

1. How do you see the idea of Pedagogical Content Knowledge expanding your role as an educator—specifically, as a co-teacher?
2. How can you and your co-teacher combine one of the co-teaching models while naturally embedding your knowledge of guiding learners to become self-motivated?
3. Discuss one lesson coming up this week or next week. How will you mindfully incorporate opportunities for students to self-motivate? How will you know they will be building their skills and strategies for this lesson—but more importantly expanding their capacity to transfer these skills to self-motivate across time and settings?
4. What is one new idea from this chapter that resonates with you at this moment in time?

Chapter 5

1. What is your current practice for incorporating emotions and self-regulation in your instructional cycle? What is your role and responsibility? What is the role and responsibility of your co-teacher?
2. What is your opinion about social emotional learning? How may you embed to optimize a risk-free learning zone with your co-teacher?
3. How could you elevate the learning process by incorporating social emotional learning with varying your application of the co-teaching models? Review the models in Chapter 1 and share one new idea.
4. Consider a student whose learning behaviors have been misunderstood for lacking motivation or effort—when it could really be a need for support with executive function skills. What is his or her specific need? How could you and your co-teacher address and redirect this student's performance?